YOUR GUIDE TO POLAND

By the same author:

YOUR GUIDE TO RUMANIA

Your Guide to
POLAND

by

TED APPLETON

FUNK & WAGNALLS
NEW YORK

Library of Congress Catalog Card
Number 68-18174

Published by Funk & Wagnalls
A Division of Reader's Digest Books, Inc.
by arrangement with Alvin Redman Limited

Printed in Great Britain by
D. R. Hillman & Sons Ltd.
Frome, Somerset

FOREWORD

As head of the Polish Travel Office in London I know the number of English-speaking visitors to my country has over the past few years shown a steady increase, as more people realise Poland is not only at the heart of Europe but embodies much that is best in European scenery, mountains, lakes, rivers and bathing beaches, as well as a unique culture.

The fact that Poland also happens to be a touristically new and unknown country considerably increases her appeal.

In this book Ted Appleton, following his travels through Poland, opens to you the heart of my country. With him you wander through our fine cities and lovely countryside, but as his narrative unfolds you also get to know my fellow countrymen and women, and end by realising some of our sacrifices and achievements in resurrecting Poland from the devastation of a war which, though it dealt harshly with Europe, in Poland reached high peaks of destructiveness and horror.

Informative, practical, friendly, lively, here is a guide book for visitors to my country and for armchair travellers seeking to widen their travel knowledge.

R. T. KOWALCZYK
Director
Poland's Travel Information Centre

5

CONTENTS

7

9

11

ILLUSTRATIONS

13

ILLUSTRATIONS

PART I

OUTLINING THE POLISH PICTURE

WITAJCIE W POLSCE—WELCOME TO POLAND

It's hard to get Poland into focus. Though in its turbulent and colourful history it has at times been one of Europe's great nations with frontiers stretching from the Baltic to the Black Sea, during the past hundred years, due to partitioning and as a battlefield in two world wars, Poland has slipped into a limbo to become a kind of never-never land you hardly think about.

Because it *is* out of focus, a visit to Poland becomes more than a holiday, it becomes a series of exciting explorations as for the enquiring visitor it sloughs off its shell revealing a young, virile people, pleasing scenery and architectural and cultural treasures of which any nation might be justifiably proud.

Do not imagine Poland a flat, uninteresting country. Parts are flat, very flat, but craggy peaks with deeply forested flanks give Poland some of Europe's loveliest if not most majestic mountains.

Then there is its Baltic coastline, with long stretches of soft sand beaches backed by dunes and woods, beaches where you can laze and bathe while small sailing craft ruffle the surface of an emerald coloured sea.

When it comes to lakes, Poland can number hers by the thousand. Some are large, almost like inland seas; others quite tiny. Most are surrounded by deep forests. Many are joined to others by gentle woodland streams. On a still summer morning when the unruffled waters reflect every tree and there is just a hint of mist above the water, their beauty is something you will find hard to forget, even if mid-summer mosquitos are a pest.

17

Poland has great rivers too. The Vistula, Bug, Odra, Warta and many others. She has castles like Malbork and Wawel, often packed with magnificent treasures. The palaces of Wilanow, Lazienki and Nieborow are treasure trove too, as well as evocative of the leisured elegance of the seventeenth and eighteenth centuries.

There are magnificent cathedrals, towns and cities where you seem able to step back into the Middle Ages and cottages with colourwashed wooden walls and deeply thatched roofs, or roofs of wooden pantiles. You can thrill to gay peasant costumes worn as everyday dress, brush away tears as you survey the tragedy of Auschwitz, feel proud to tread the streets of Warsaw, which, having thrown aside her tears and ashes, seems to grow before your eyes and will one day be a beautiful city. Great factories like those of Nowa Huta herald the beginning of a new industrial era, while the salt mines of Wieliczka and the Cloth Hall of Cracow recall Poland's former economic importance.

Everywhere you go, in towns and villages, you will find vast armies of workmen putting up new buildings. The new city apartment blocks are particularly eye-catching with their balcony walls painted in gay yellow and orange colours, which caught by the northern sunshine cause the whole building to glow with Mediterranean colour. Look in at the windows. You will find living rooms like exotic gardens packed tight with flowering plants. How the Poles love their flowers!

Comfortable hotels offer every modern amenity. Polish food is plain but plentiful, and there's always lashings of fresh cream for those who want it.

The Poles love music—any kind of music. Even the smaller hotels have bands playing western tunes for dancing. In the international hotels you will find restaurant dance bands and coffee room pianists. In fact a gay musical tradition wells up from the students' cellar clubs to the big hotels.

Then there are the Poles themselves, hospitable, genuinely pleased to meet you and go out of their way to talk to you. They are the most elegant of Eastern European peoples, the women slavishly copying western fashion, the lounge-suited men neatly groomed even if in summer they do favour sling-back sandals. When you look at the cost of clothes this elegance is not the least among Poland's many miracles. And look at the people's hands. Even those of workmen are beautifully manicured.

The Poles are honest too. In all our Polish travelling only once, in Zakopane, were we cheated and then by a merry-faced rogue of a fiacre driver who did the deed with such an impish twinkle that we almost forgave him. Taxi drivers, shopkeepers, waiters are meticulous in ensuring you are not short-changed. We had the hardest job getting anyone to accept even the smallest tip.

The Poles admit their language is impossible to understand, but many speak English, French or German, so you have little difficulty in making yourself understood, though before speaking German it is courteous to let it be known you are English, for Poland's war wounds still sting.

Full of ideas about the Communist system of government, you will be surprised to find Sunday church-going the event of the week with every seat filled, people crowding the aisles and erupting on to the church steps, unable for the crowds to get inside. Priests and nuns are everywhere. Every peasant cottage has an altar or a series of sacred pictures. In Poland, religion is a living thing.

Though you will see no signs of real poverty, you will meet beggars who must be among the most prosperous

Poles. We spent some time watching a beggar at work outside a church. It appeared to us that at least 50 per cent of those who passed slipped a coin into his hand. Local peasants seemed more generous than the townsfolk; not one peasant passed without giving him something.

We watched second-hand clothes pedlars do wonderful business in street markets, especially if selling clothes of nylon or other manmade fibres. But we also saw hats made of sable fur costing far more than we could afford being snapped up in Warsaw milliners' shops.

Everywhere we looked was something to interest us. Giant paper cut-outs of flowers and animals pasted to kindergarten windows. Ancient buildings wrecked by war and carefully reassembled from the rubble so it was almost impossible to notice they were fake. Toto kiosks where you could fill in forms similar to our football coupons and if lucky win yourself a fortune.

We saw men drink numberless glasses of vodka and walk away quite steadily as though they had spent the evening drinking water. We tried the ritual of afternoon tea served without milk in thin glass tumblers which were too hot to handle, ate Polish breakfasts of sliced cheese on lean ham, and boiled eggs broken into a glass tumbler standing in a dish of warm water to keep the eggs hot while you ate them.

Interest was the keynote of our Polish journey—an interest woven into the varied fabric of Poland's everyday life, a country which says 'Witajcie W Polsce—Welcome to Poland'; an invitation you should readily accept.

A SHORT HISTORY OF POLAND

It's not certain when the Poles, a Slav tribe and

20

kinsmen to the Russians and Czechs, arrived in Poland. A reference of A.D. 552 vaguely mentions a Slav tribe living on the banks of the River Vistula.

The first recorded historical event was in A.D. 963 when tribute was paid by Prince Mieszko to the Roman Emperor Otho. Two years later Prince Mieszko became a Christian.

Guided by St. Adalbert he and his people accepted the teachings of the Roman Church to which they have clung despite every vicissitude. Today 64 per cent of Poles are Roman Catholic. Converted by Rome and not by the Orthodox Church centred on Constantinople, for the first time in her history Poland looked west instead of east, an outlook which throughout history has caused her considerable trouble with her eastern neighbours.

Boleslas (A.D. 992–1025), son of Mieszko and a friend of the Roman Emperor Otho III, was the first Pole to be given the title of king. His reign was by no means peaceful, with wars against Henry II of Germany and the Grand Duke of Kiev.

From the very beginning Poland's political system was based on the theory of personal liberty. Though most of the liberties were in the hands of the ruling class, at a time when the word liberty meant little outside Poland it was a progressive step. Much of Poland's political troubles stemmed from attempts to put the theory into practice. Their kings, denied the right to hereditary rule, were elected by a majority vote of the ruling class. This resulted in a sorry procession of Polish monarchs, many of them foreigners given the throne because they agreed to support nobility rule and privilege.

In the Polish Parliament the idea of individual liberty produced the absurd 'liberum veto'. If any one man objected to a proposed legislation the bill was immediately thrown out even though the majority were in favour. The 'liberum veto' gave the privileged a whip hand which they wielded through centuries of Polish history with disastrous results for the country.

Casimir (A.D. 1040–1058), grandson of Boleslas, eager to ensure that all his people remained Christian, encouraged foreign monks to settle in Poland. This political move strengthened a young kingdom surrounded by Christian States who would have welcomed the pretext of Polish heathenism to invade the country.

Boleslas II, son of Casimir, suspicious of the churches' growing power, quarrelled with Stanislaus Bishop of Cracow and killed him. Put under an interdict by Pope Gregory VII Boleslas was driven from Poland.

This was disastrous for the young country. Although Ladislaus brother of Boleslas was crowned, the Pope would not ratify his regal title, so for 200 years Poland was no more than a duchy.

Boleslas III (A.D. 1102–1139) a powerful prince increased Poland's size, though at his death his sons divided the country between them into small dukedoms and principalities. Casimir (A.D. 1177–1194) reunited the country and called a council at Leczyca to hammer out some kind of constitution which would form a basis for the first Polish Parliament. For several centuries, among European nations only Poland and England had a form of Parliamentary government.

An eastern outpost of western civilisation, Poland's geographical position attracted migratory armies who constantly crossed her borders to ravage the country. Poland accepted this situation knowing herself to be the springboard for the spread of Christianity eastwards.

In A.D. 1241 the Tartars swept into Poland looting, burning and murdering. Poland's neighbours—the

Lithuanians and Prussians—also decided to take a hand. In desperation Conrad, Duke of Masovia, asked the Order of Teutonic Knights for help.

This strange German semi-religious society of knights, priests and serving brothers had been formed by the merchants of Bremen and Lubeck to look after the sick, widows and orphans, to protect the Church and to fight the heathen in the Holy Land. But the Holy Land was a long way off while the heathen living on the rich lands to the east of Germany were ripe for some knightly activity.

Having accepted Conrad's invitation and defeated the Prussian invaders, the Teutonic Knights turned on the Poles, annexed the Province of Pomerania, forcing the Poles into serfdom. They then invited large numbers of Germans to settle the Polish lands and initiated a problem which in our own time erupted into the Second World War.

Under Casimir III (A.D. 1333–1370), known as Casimir the Great, Poland achieved greatness as Casimir made certain that he held the real authority. To combat a coalition of the Teutonic Knights and the Bohemian rulers, Casimir allied himself with Hungary's Anjou dynasty. In 1364 he founded Cracow university, built a network of roads, and reformed the Polish currency. It was a tragedy for Poland when Casimir died early after a fall from his horse.

During the reign of Casimir the Great Poland entered upon her 'Golden Age' which lasted for 200 years—an age noted for its liberal thought with Poland a peaceful oasis in which the arts flourished while Europe was torn apart by wars. During this period her political role was to champion small nations who sought her protection.

Casimir was succeeded by Louis of Hungary (A.D. 1370–1382) the son of his sister Elizabeth. A great figure in Hungarian history, Louis made little impact on Poland, though his daughter Jadwiga's marriage to Jagiello of Lithuania, which at that time was a considerable nation ruling the Russian tribes as far east as Kiev and the River Dnieper, strengthened Poland's position.

The principal event of this period was the defeat on the 15th August 1410 of the Teutonic Knights at the great battle of Tannenberg. The knights never recovered from this defeat. Weakened as a military force their power diminished though they clung to the Province of Pomerania.

The next Jagiello to reign was the youthful Wladislaw who embroiled himself in Hungarian and Turkish affairs and was killed in 1444 at the Battle of Varna. He was succeeded by Casimir the Jagiellon (A.D. 1447–1492), who waited three years to be crowned.

In 1446 by treaty with the Teutonic Knights Casimir regained the Provinces of West Prussia and Pomerania with the cities of Gdansk and Torun. The Grand Master of the Teutonic Order, Albert of Hohenzollern, whose descendants included the last German Kaiser, agreed to do homage to the Polish king in return for the Duchy of East Prussia and the right to use a black eagle for his insignia—an insignia which became the hated German eagle.

During Casimir's reign the Statute of Nieszawa turned Poland's government into an oligarchy of nobles. Though this may sound undemocratic, at that time no less than 5 per cent of the Polish nation were in the 'slachta' or nobility class. Their cultural influence was considerable even though they resisted social change. Bearing in mind that at that time in England only 2 per cent of the population had voting rights, Poland with a 5 per cent representation could be considered the most progressive nation of the period.

John Albert (A.D. 1492–1501) succeeded Casimir. Harsh laws were introduced binding the peasants to the soil. To ensure peasant subjugation merchants who might have influenced them were denied the right to buy land. Even so, with many landowners being a kind of father figure to their serfs, the lot of the Polish peasant was considerably better than in other European countries.

In 1497 John Albert was deposed and the Polish throne given to his brother Alexander (A.D. 1501–1506), married to Helen, daughter of Ivan III of Russia. Russia was now actively drawn into the Polish political arena.

Succeeding Alexander, Sigismund I (A.D. 1506–1548) found himself faced with the Reformation which was sweeping across Europe. Some of his ministers worked out a programme of reform based on the Protestant ideology, not from any love for the new faith, but as a means of curtailing the growing power of the Roman Catholic Church which had considerable influence with the peasants who looked to the priest for advice. In Poland the only positive result of the Reformation was legislation preventing state authorities from carrying out sentences pronounced by ecclesiastical courts.

In 1514 latent hostility between Poles and Russians erupted when the Russians seized the border city of Smolensk and claimed Lithuanian territory.

Lithuania with close Polish alliances looked to Poland for help and the duel between Russia and Poland destined to bedevil so much of Poland's later history began.

The Lublin Union of 1569 drew Poland and Lithuania closer together—but the Russian threat, with Poland needing to deploy troops to protect her eastern border, so weakened her position that when threatened by the

Hapsburgs, Poland had to relinquish Bohemia and Hungary which at that time were ruled by the Polish king.

Cracow being considered too isolated for the new Polish–Lithuanian union, Warsaw was chosen to be Poland's new capital.

The Jagiello dynasty ended in 1572 with the death of Sigismund II. The nobles now offered the crown to Henry of Valois, brother to King Charles IX of France, provided he would swear to respect the prerogatives of the Polish nobility. Known as the 'Pacta Conventa' it was to be demanded from every subsequent Polish sovereign.

Henry of Valois accepted the crown and ruled Poland for five months. When Charles IX of France died suddenly, Henry hurried from Poland to claim the French crown, leaving Poland without a ruler for the next six years until Stephen Batory (A.D. 1578–1586) a Transylvanian Prince married to Anna, sister of the last Jagiellon King Sigismund II, was elected.

Stephen Batory was a vigorous, intelligent man. He was not afraid to take on Russia and went so far as to annex the Province of Livonia (part of Latvia and Estonia) to bar Russian access to the Baltic. He might have succeeded, only Sweden and Denmark were also interested and the Livonian adventure ended with the division of the disputed area among all contestants.

Stephen Batory tried unsuccessfully to check the power of the Polish nobility. He founded the University of Vilna and strengthened the Polish Church by introducing the Jesuits to Poland. Protestantism which had made little headway among Polish peasants lost its impetus and went into decline.

On Stephen Batory's death, Sigismund III (A.D. 1587–1632) was elected. Son of the Swedish king, he

26

tried to unite Poland and Sweden but his fanatical Roman Catholicism was unacceptable to the Protestant Swedes and his reign degenerated into a series of wars.

The Russian dynasty having died out Sigismund claimed the Russian throne. At first his efforts to rule in Russia were successful, his son Ladislaus being crowned Tsar by a powerful section of the Russian nobility.

As fanatical a Roman Catholic as his father, Ladislaus was quickly unpopular among Orthodox Russians. Under considerable political pressure in 1618 the Poles abandoned claims to the Russian throne.

Roman Catholicism also caused Sigismund to lose the Swedish throne. In an effort to recover his Swedish crown, in 1605 Sigismund declared war on Sweden. The Swedes retaliated by invading Poland, capturing Livonia, Gdansk and Pomerania and held on to them for thirty years.

One outcome of the Swedish wars was Poland's surrender of Prussia to the Brandenburg-Hohenzollern family who having united the Provinces of Brandenburg and Prussia constituted a new threat to Poland.

Sigismund, desperate for help, guaranteed to surrender his Polish crown to the influential Hapsburg dynasty if they would help him win the throne of Sweden. This upset the Turks who were at war with the Hapsburgs, and they promptly invaded Poland. Their advance was only halted after two terrible battles.

Almost friendless due to Sigismund's foolishness and with the country weakened by his wars, the Polish nobility increased their powers and caused considerable trouble in the previously peaceful Ukraine.

The Ukrainians—a Slav tribe—had been successfully and peacefully ruled by the Polish and Lithuanian kings. An intelligent, cultured people, they resented a new Polish policy introduced by the nobility and designed to turn the Ukrainians into peasant serfs. A series of isolated Ukrainian uprisings became a full-scale rebellion, to which was added religious conflict as the Roman Catholic Poles strove to again subjugate the Orthodox Ukrainians. The reign of Ladislaus son of Sigismund (A.D. 1632–1648) was occupied in trying to sort out the Ukrainian problem.

Ladislaus was succeeded by John Casimir (A.D. 1648–1668). He too was caught up in the continuing Ukrainian turmoil, the Russians seeing the possibility of territorial gain helping the Ukrainians in their fight. In 1667 the Ukrainian revolt ended with the Ukraine partitioned between Russia and Poland, the River Dnieper being the line of demarcation. This gave Poland a further minority problem which would only be resolved by future bloodshed.

The Ukrainian wars had exhausted Poland so that when in 1655 Charles Gustavus X of Sweden invaded Poland with an army of 60,000 he captured both Warsaw and Cracow with little trouble. The Polish serfs though slaves of the nobility now displayed the patriotism which so many times in subsequent centuries was to surprise Europe. In a nation-wide revolt inspired by the heroic defence of the monastery at Czestochowa they fought the Swedish forces and in the end achieved victory with the Polish–Swedish Treaty of 1660 which gave each country the right to retain its pre-war possessions. As a reward for his services during the Swedish invasions, the Poles gave the vassal Prince of Brandenburg full independent rights to the Province of Prussia which was now entirely lost to Poland and destined in time to become one of the great powers which would partition the country from which it sprang.

In 1668 John Casimir abdicated and was succeeded by Michael Wisniowiecki (A.D. 1669–1673) who sat helpless as the Turks swarmed into Poland to capture the city of Kamieniec Podolsk. To stop the Turks Poland agreed to pay them a yearly tribute but found this did not stop the Turks from invading the Ukraine.

A Polish nobleman, John Sobieski, met and defeated the Turks at the Battle of Chocim (1673) and Michael Wisniowiecki having died Sobieski was offered the Polish crown. A man of great character, John Sobieski (A.D. 1674–1696) might have done a great deal for Poland but his entire reign was wasted fighting the Turks. His most noteworthy achievement apart from being the great-grandfather to Bonnie Prince Charlie was in 1683 when he raised the Turkish siege of Vienna to prevent a major Turkish invasion of Western Europe.

On June 17th 1696, prematurely worn out, John Sobieski died. Though his Turkish victories saved Europe they had destroyed Poland which politically and economically was in a vulnerable position.

The Poles chose Frederick Augustus of Saxony (A.D. 1697–1733) as Sobieski's successor. A coarse, ignorant man who believed in the doctrine of absolute monarchy, he allied Poland with Russia to go to war with Sweden.

Charles XII of Sweden having first defeated the Danes and Russians invaded Poland, defeated her army and banished Frederick Augustus, replacing him with Stanislaus Leszcynski, a bitter opponent of Frederick's policies. Victory for Charles XII did not last long. The Russians stormed back, defeated the Swedes and Frederick Augustus was back on the Polish throne. Denied popular Polish support Frederick Augustus held on to the throne only by Russian support given by Tsar Peter I (Peter the Great).

As a sideline to this war, the Prince of Brandenburg

with a sense of destiny invested himself with the title of King of Prussia and reached a political settlement with Russia to ensure Poland would be kept weak and denied any sort of reform which might rally her to again become a European political force.

Poland's next rulers, tools of the Russians, allowed Poland in 1772 to be partitioned for the first time between Russia, Prussia and Austria, the Prussians seizing the Baltic Coast.

The loss of their access to the sea gave the Poles a moral shock. Their political weakness was now apparent to the humblest peasant while they were shocked to realise their military might consisted of no more than 14,000 miserably armed men. In two centuries of mismanagement Poland had toppled from a powerful and envied nation to become a football for lesser nations to carve up and play with.

In 1792 a remarkable session of the Polish Parliament gave the Polish towns the right of self-government, a consultative voice in any future Parliaments and sought to ease the lot of the depressed Polish peasantry. It also made the nomination of Poland's future rulers hereditary rather than a political nomination.

Though most Poles knew this action was being taken far too late they rallied behind this Parliament. Afraid that it might curtail their power, later in the year at the Conference of Targovica, the Polish nobility rejected this new constitution, one of the most enlightened documents to have come from any Parliamentary assembly of the age, and more enlightened than that of Revolutionary France which was to be published several months later.

Poland's enemies—Prussia, Russia and Austria— fearing the thwarted Poles might rise against the nobility and follow the French revolutionary pattern, resolved on Poland's final destruction. Troops poured across her borders. The final struggle for Polish national life was now taking place which culminated in the famous Diet of Grodno in 1793.

Afraid for their future should the militant merchant and peasant classes rally, the Polish nobility called in Russian troops who surrounded the meeting place frightening those members of the opposition who had not already sold themselves to the aristocracy for money. So the Polish nobility took an active part in Poland's second partitioning.

Enraged by this betrayal, in March 1794 the humbler Poles who never lacked patriotism revolted against the partitioning powers, first in Cracow where they defeated the Austrians, then in Warsaw where the Russians were driven from the capital. All over Poland peasants left the land to take up arms. Many of those responsible for the Grodno betrayal were seized and publicly executed. The revolt was followed by a Proclamation of Polance promising the peasants freedom and a better living standard.

The revolt was short-lived; Warsaw retaken and the country in the grip of famine, the peasants drifted back to their holdings and the remainder of the insurgents capitulated. Afraid that this could again happen, the occupying powers partitioned Poland yet again. Prussia now took the heart of the country including Warsaw. Austria secured Cracow and the lands between the Rivers Bug and Vistula. Russia was more than satisfied with Lithuania and the territories beyond the Bug. Poland had at last been wiped clean off the European map.

In adversity Poland, very much like Britain, seems to achieve her true greatness. Awakening to a nightmare of occupation, tyranny and oppression in which even the Polish language was forbidden in the Prussian zone, Polish patriotism welled up like a fountain, the Polish belief in personal liberty became the consuming passion in every man, woman and child. Polish cultural and economic life revived while guerrilla tactics were used against the occupying powers as the Poles sought to regain independence.

Those who had left the country organised Polish Freedom Legions. It was all very reminiscent of Polish activities during the last war.

Poles living abroad saw in Napoleon a hope for Poland's future. In 1806, having defeated the Central Powers, Napoleon created the Duchy of Warsaw from territory reclaimed from Austria and Prussia. Napoleon also went part way to liberating the Polish peasant, but before all his plans could be put into operation his attention was distracted and he had far more to think about than Poland's future.

Following his Russian retreat of 1812, Russia overran Poland and was hard on the heels of Napoleon who had been joined by the small Polish army who were finally cut to pieces in 1813 at the Battle of Leipzig.

But Napoleon's activities had brought Poland's plight to the attention of the victorious allies. In 1814 at the Congress of Vienna most of Napoleon's Duchy of Warsaw was formed into the autonomous Kingdom of Poland protected by Alexander I of Russia. Cracow and its neighbourhood was declared a republic under the protection of the three original partitioning powers— Russia, Austria and Prussia who between them still held a great deal of the dismembered country.

Some sort of a nation once more, the merchant and peasant classes found conditions had hardly improved. The old families were still in power. Though they set about improving their vast estates, these improvements

1. Warsaw—the Market Square in the Old Town

2. The Lazienki Palace, Warsaw

3. Warsaw—the Castle Square, with the Column to King Sigismund III

4. The Mermaid—symbol of Warsaw

rarely reached peasant level.

The nineteenth century Industrial Revolution brought changes to Poland, though it was slower than in other countries. The abolition of customs barriers betweeen Russia and the tiny Polish State opened vast markets to the Polish merchant class.

But the freedom-loving Poles were far from happy with the situation. Under Russian protection they lived in what could only be described as a 'police state' with the ever watchful Russians ready to destroy any liberation movements.

On 29th November 1830, led by cadets of the Warsaw Cadet School, open insurrection took place against the Russians. It lasted for six months and was suppressed with such barbarities that thousands of Poles fled to England, France, Germany and Belgium where they continued to work for the liberation of Poland which had been swallowed up by Russia.

Further insurrections took place in 1848 and 1863, but denied outside support the Poles were quickly cut to pieces by the Russian army.

Caught up in the Russian revolutionary movements of 1905–1907 Polish workers struck in many important Polish cities, but the strikes soon failed. In the Prussian zone pressure on the subject Poles continued. Poles were even denied the right to build houses. The Prussians were determined to Germanise Poland's western provinces no matter what it might cost the Poles living there.

In 1918 at the end of the first World War with Germany, with the Germans and Austrians defeated and the Russians bogged down by their revolution, Poland was again given independence.

The Poles at once set about raising their pitifully low living standards. Unfortunately the task was great, much remained undone and the needed agrarian reforms were never carried out. Polish industry continued inadequate while her politicians though aware of the Nazi menace somehow failed to grasp the full extent of the German threat to their country.

When on September 1st 1939 the Nazis invaded Poland, the country was almost powerless to resist aggression by the world's finest fighting machine. Though the ordinary people rallied to defend their country fighting beside their troops, from the outset German victory in Poland was assured. Within weeks Poland was occupied as far as the River Bug.

Poland now found herself subjected to a bestiality such as the world had never dreamed possible. But again Polish men, women and children rose to heights of greatness and courage in a period of national martyrdom. Though with their concentration camps, public executions, collective responsibility campaigns which gave the Germans the right to wipe out entire communities if one man showed resistance, not to mention the Jewish massacres, the Nazis strove to subjugate Poland, they only succeeded in fanning Polish patriotism to white heat.

Men, women and elder children banded themselves into guerrilla units hiding out in the forests and fighting hundreds of battles and skirmishes pinning down German troops and disrupting communications with the Russian front. In 1943 the Jewish revolt in the Warsaw Ghetto kept the Nazis fighting for weeks.

The Warsaw Rising on 1st August 1944 when almost the entire city fought the Nazi tyrants will forever rank among the finest testimonies of love for liberty no matter what the personal cost.

On the 9th May 1945 Germany capitulated having systematically and ruthlessly destroyed vast areas of

Poland and many of her finest cities.

But before Germany's final defeat Poland had planned her future. On 21st July 1944 a Polish Committee of National Liberation, set up in the recently liberated town of Chelm, put into operation plans for the reconstruction of their war-devastated country.

But of course history is continually being written. Today some of Poland's former eastern territories are in the Soviet Union, though her western frontiers have been extended so Poland now holds the Provinces of Pomerania and Silesia which have been shuttled backwards and forwards between Poland and Germany from those early days when the Teutonic Knights in their black armour thundered for the first time across the plains into Polish history to leave a legacy which has by no means been resolved.

Historically a great and powerful nation, who knows the day could come again when Poland regains some of her past greatness. The faith of her people deserves it.

PART II
ALL YOU WANT TO KNOW WHEN PLANNING YOUR HOLIDAY

RAIL TRAVEL IN POLAND

Though Poland now has a well developed railway system internal rail journeys seem endless—though they are not all that far in distance covered. On average it takes about five hours to do two hundred miles—which means that if you are travelling by rail between centres, every time you move you can reckon a day out of your holiday.

This is a great pity, for Polish rail fares are among the most reasonable in Europe. Here are a few of the more important which will help you in planning your Polish journey.

From–To	1st Class Single	2nd Class Single
Warsaw–Gdansk	$ 7.28	$4.83
Warsaw–Cracow	$ 7.14	$4.72
Warsaw–Poznan	$ 6.93	$4.65
Warsaw–Szczecin	$10.22	$6.86
Warsaw–Wroclaw	$ 8.82	$5.88
Warsaw–Sopot	$ 7.42	$4.97
Poznan–Gdansk	$ 6.86	$4.55
Poznan–Wroclaw	$ 4.34	$2.87
Cracow–Zakopane	$ 3.99	$2.73

Children between 4 and 10 years travel at half price. Over 10 years they pay full fare.

COACH TRAVEL

Two British travel agents—Fregata Travel Ltd., 100, Dean Street, London, W.1 and Anglo-Polish

Enterprises Ltd., 12, Cecil Court, London, W.C.2—have scheduled coach services between London and Poland.

Fregata's coach travellers fly from Southend to Rotterdam and have an overnight coach journey through Germany in both directions, whereas Anglo-Polish Enterprises Ltd. do the crossing by ship either to Ostend or the Hook of Holland but offer a night hotel stop in each direction with the cost for bed, breakfast and dinner being covered by the ticket.

The price for a return ticket by coach from London to Poznan by either operator is around $59.

Once in Poland you will find an excellent network of long distance coaches, these linking most of the main Polish cities. Fares are similar to those for 2nd Class rail travel. You will often find it quicker to travel by coach. For example the rail journey from Cracow to Zakopane can take the best part of five hours, whereas travelling by coach you can get there in half the time.

TRAFFIC SIGNS

Poland uses the international road traffic signs.

TRAFFIC REGULATIONS

(*a*) Drive on the right.

(*b*) Overtake on the left.

(*c*) In built-up areas cars coming from the right have priority.

(*d*) The sounding of horns is forbidden in built-up areas.

(*e*) Overtake trams on the right.

(*f*) There are no speed limits except in built-up areas where it is set at 50 kilometres (35 miles) an hour.

PETROL

There are two grades of petrol. Ordinary grade (70 octanes) costs around 4.80 zlotys (about 20 c.) a litre. Super grade (87 octanes) is 6 zlotys (about 25 c.) a litre. Oil—that known as 'extra' oil is the one to ask for—costs 25 zlotys (about $1.04) a litre.

PETROL COUPONS

You can get a 30 per cent reduction on Polish petrol prices by buying petrol coupons before you travel, at the frontier posts as you drive into Poland, at Orbis Hotels throughout Poland or at one of the branches of the Polish Motor Touring Office.

A book of 10 coupons costs about $7.28 but each coupon will buy: $3\frac{1}{2}$ litres of 87 octane petrol or 4 litres of 80 octane petrol, or 5 litres of 70 octane petrol, or 1 litre of 'Extra' lubrication oil.

PETROL STATIONS

There is no shortage of petrol stations on the main Polish trunk roads. Most of them open about 8.00 a.m. and close around 5.00 p.m. so be warned and carry some spare petrol with you. In the main provincial cities you will usually find one all-night petrol station but you are not always going to be in a main provincial city —so try to keep the tank topped up.

SERVICING STATIONS

Servicing stations (TOS) are state operated. They can do all the running repairs your car is likely to need. You will find plenty of them in the main cities and along the main tourist routes, and a very high standard of

41

efficiency can be expected from them. Most cities also have privately owned servicing stations.

MOTORING ASSOCIATIONS

The Polish Motoring Association (PZM) has its head office in Warsaw at Nowy Swiat 35 (Telephone 26-42-11) as well as branches at the principal frontier points and in the main provincial cities.

The Polski Zwiazek Motorowy Office, Krucza Avenue 6/14, Warsaw will help you with your itinerary, insurance etc.

CALCULATING ROAD DISTANCES

Poland uses the metric system to measure distance.

1 metre equals 3.28 feet or 39.37 inches. 1 kilometre is equal to 1093.614 yards or five-eighths of a mile or nearly five furlongs.

Here is a short table of kilometric distances with their equivalents in miles.

Kilometres	Miles	Kilometres	Miles
5	3⅛	29	18
13	8	33	20½
17	10½	37	23
21	13	45	28
25	15½	50	31⅛

MEAN TIME

From June to October Polish official time is two hours fast on Greenwich Mean Time. In winter it is only one hour ahead.

CLIMATE

Poland's climate can only be described as variable— which, like our own, covers anything. It is a mixture of

Eastern Europe's Continental climate and the Oceanic climate of Western Europe. The advantage of this mixture is that Poland seems to have six distinct seasons against the usual four seasons of other parts of Europe.

In winter Poland is not quite so cold as the Soviet Union, but it is cold enough. There is plenty of snow, especially in the mountains, while the rivers and lakes are icebound. Temperatures range from −4 degrees to 32 degrees Fahrenheit. Winter starts in December and lasts until about the end of February. It is succeeded by the early spring when the snows begin to melt. Though temperatures rise sharply (from 32–41 degrees Fahrenheit) this period is seldom longer than three weeks and is followed by a normal spring which gets under way about the end of March and continues through to the end of May. Travellers will find this a good period to see Poland. At this time of the year the weather is normally settled and at times it can be quite warm, though you can also be put out by sudden sharp frosts which can strike as late as May.

Summer with temperatures from 59–85 degrees Fahrenheit can produce hot clear sunny days, though you can also get rain—rain being a summer feature of countries with a Continental climate—so pack a mac with all those summery clothes.

Autumn usually gets the year's best weather. September and October are beautiful settled months with a succession of fine sunny days with temperatures hovering around 41–59 degrees Fahrenheit.

Towards the end of October Poland is in the grip of early winter frosts which continue through November. Cold winds from Russia cause the thermometer to plummet to around 30 degrees Fahrenheit. Towards the end of November the cold winds drop and heavy snowfalls are then to be expected with a further fall in

43

temperatures. The moment the snow comes the year's climatic cycle is completed.

In the mountains conditions are always a little different. In the mountains you can expect the heaviest summer rainfall, while during the winter months conditions are ideal for ski-ing from late October to May.

Warsaw and the Central plains have similar summer temperatures as we do, while the rainfall, around 22 inches, is the same as London.

Here is a table of the average daily Fahrenheit temperatures of Warsaw. The first figure indicates the average daily minimum followed by the average maximum.

Month	City–Warsaw
January	25–30
February	27–32
March	35–41
April	46–54
May	57–67
June	63–72
July	65–75
August	64–73
September	57–65
October	47–54
November	36–40
December	29–32

June to September is considered to be the Polish holiday season—though in the mountains there is also a winter season lasting from the end of December to March.

PASSPORT AND VISAS

Travellers entering Poland must hold a valid passport stamped with a Polish visa.

44

There are no less than *FIVE* different types of Polish visas—so make sure you know just which one you want when asking for visa application forms from the Polish Consulate or from your travel agent.

Tourist Visas require two application forms, two photographs and a tourist voucher from your travel agent showing the number of days you have booked in Poland and paid for. Visa fee (1968) $4.13.

Standard Visas issued for business or official visits still need two application forms and two photographs, though this time they must be accompanied by your official invitation confirming that accommodation is being provided, otherwise you will need a travel agent's voucher showing you have booked and paid for accommodation. There are two standard visas. One has a validity of up to 30 days and costs $8.54, the other up to 90 days costing $12.04.

CUSTOMS REGULATIONS

At the time of going to print (1966) these are the regulations in force—but like most regulations they can be changed, so it is wise to check before you go.

You can take in and out of Poland duty free:

Personal effects required during the holiday, such as clothing, underwear, shoes, toilet accessories, travelling rugs, books and other articles of everyday use.

Jewellery for personal use. The total weight of gold, platinum, precious stones and fine pearls taken in must not exceed 1.6 troy ounces.

A portable radio, camera, or amateur 8 or 16 mm cine camera.

Photographic plates for ten pictures or five rolls of cine film (200 feet) for the camera or cine camera taken by you into Poland.

Hunting and sporting guns provided a permit has previously been obtained. 100 rounds of ammunition for hunting and sporting guns and up to 25 rounds for hand arms.

Medicines in quantities required for the holiday.

Up to 13 lbs. 4 ozs. of foodstuffs for the journey, but not more than 2 lbs. 3 ozs. of chocolate or chocolate products.

Alcoholic beverages up to 2 litres including 0.5 litres of spirits per person over 17 years of age.

Up to 200 cigarettes or 50 cigars or 9 ounces of tobacco for every person over 17 years of age.

Small musical instruments, small tools, wheel chairs, prams, and gifts with an import duty not exceeding 1,500 zlotys.

All items of personal value for which you claim exemption have to be entered on a combined Customs and Currency Declaration Form, though it is not necessary to itemise clothing. The form is stamped by the customs official at the point of entry and must be carefully kept as you will need to show it when leaving Poland, only then it will include details of all purchases made in the country. Again the form will be examined. Only when it has been stamped and withdrawn by the customs man at your exit point from Poland will your baggage be cleared.

CURRENCY REGULATIONS

You can take as much currency and travellers' cheques as you like into Poland, provided that you do not infringe our own currency regulations, which must when applying for travellers' cheques be checked with your bank or travel agent.

The amount of money and travellers' cheques on you has to be entered on the Currency Declaration Form which you will get from the customs when entering Poland.

Every time you change money or travellers' cheques you must show your passport and countersign a receipt showing the amount in currency notes or travellers' cheques being changed into Polish currency at that time. A copy of the receipt is given to you to be shown when paying your hotel bill and on leaving the country.

The reason for this precaution is that in Poland there is a flourishing currency Black Market. During our journey we were several times offered some very fanciful exchange rates if we had cared to part with some of our bank notes. It is of course illegal to trade on the Black Market; if caught punishment is stiff. In any case zlotys are valueless outside Poland even if they could be exported. Zlotys spent on souvenirs are checked against the amount of travellers' cheques and currency changed by you to ensure that no illegal currency transactions have been carried out by you. If you do want a currency bonus for your travellers' cheques, you can get it in the shape of Orbis currency coupons.

Though you get 23.95 zlotys to the $1, this is not a particularly good rate of exchange.

In order to stimulate tourism, Orbis have introduced special currency coupons for tourists who change no less than $20 in travellers' cheques or sterling notes at a time, increasing purchasing power by 66%.

Each time we changed $28, in addition to the 670 zlotys received in currency notes and coins, we also got currency coupons to the value of 420 zlotys.

We soon found these coupons to be of considerable value to us and not a meaningless 'gimmick' as we had first supposed. We used them to pay for petrol, hotel accommodation, restaurant meals, drinks in the hotel and when we went shopping we learned to look for those shops with a window sticker labelled 'coupons' which meant that they could be exchanged for souvenirs. In fact most of the presents brought home were bought in this way.

We also discovered that if the total value of the coupon was not being spent, we would be given change not in the form of low value coupons but in coins or notes.

Orbis coupons are issued at all Orbis currency exchange offices, at the offices of the Polish Automobile and Motorcycle Federation and at border stations.

While one does not look a gift horse in the mouth and these currency coupons did help to make our visit less expensive, we could not help feeling that it would have been much simpler to give us a realistic exchange rate in the first place, rather than that we should go around offering 100 zloty coupons for 20 zloty purchases in order to get 80 zlotys in cash to augment our supply so we would not be limited to 'coupon' shops and restaurants.

No Polish currency notes or coins can be taken out of Poland. If at the end of your holiday you have any Polish currency left the customs office at the point of departure takes it into safe keeping and gives you a deposit note. The sum deposited can be withdrawn at any time within a period of one year from the date of deposit otherwise it is lost.

In other words during your last days in Poland run your currency down and hesitate before you change any more travellers' cheques, or change small denomination cheques. If you have any notes over when leaving the country, do as we did and give it to the taxi driver or courier.

Polish Money

The standard unit of Polish currency is the zloty which is made up of 100 groszy. Banknotes are issued in denominations of 500, 100, 50, 20 zlotys and coins for 10, 5, 2 and 1 zloty as well as for 50, 20, 10 and 5 groszy.

Rate of Exchange

There are at the present time (1968) 23.95 zlotys to $1. 11.98 zlotys = 50 c.; 6 zlotys = 25 c.; 2.40 zlotys = 10 c.

Orbis—The Polish Travel Office

Most matters concerning Polish tourism are in the hands of Orbis. Not only is it the largest travel organisation in Poland, it is the oldest.

There is a network of Orbis offices spread across Poland. The best Polish hotels are Orbis establishments. They have the best coaches, arrange car hire, book theatre, cinema and concert tickets, lay on fishing and hunting trips and also have currency exchange facilities in most of their principal hotels and branch offices. It is through this organisation that most travel agents and tourists deal.

We found Orbis very reliable and we were never once let down. Their representatives were perfect linguists as well as good hosts. Nothing seemed too much trouble for them. They never seemed tired of our company or the company of other travellers entrusted to their care. Though they were up early and always last to bed they never appeared to be tired and their good humour was infectious. Their patriotism was heartwarming, and their knowledge of all things Polish phenomenal, and at times they had to put up with some difficult questioning from people who would not be fobbed off with half answers. Not that the guides tried to do this, except in cases where the question was obviously facetious or in poor taste. Even then, they still managed to keep good-humoured.

In fact memories of our Polish guides are some of our warmest recollections and we are pleased to count more than one among our friends.

Here is a list of addresses of the Orbis offices in the principal towns. You can call at any of these addresses for information or to arrange excursions. Those with currency exchange facilities are marked (c).

Orbis Head Office
Bracka 16, Warsaw. Phone 26-02-71

London Office
313, Regent Street, London, W.1. Phone LANgham 8381.

Warsaw (c)
Avenue Krakowskie Przedmiescie 13. Phone 26-75-14.

Bialystok (c)
Rynek Kosciuszki 13. Phone 58-52.

Cracow (c)
Szczepanski Square 3. Phone 240-33.

Czestochowa (c)
11 Aleja 16. Phone 20-56.

Elblag (c)
Avenue 1 Maja 1. Phone 20-61.

Gdansk (c)
Gorkiego Square 1. Phone 31-14-66.

Gdynia (c)
Avenue Swietojanska 36. Phone 21-68-25.

Jelenia Gora (c)
Avenue 15 Grudnia 36. Phone 22-07.

Katowice (c)
Rynek 1. Phone 368-20.

Kielce (c)
Avenue Sienkiewicza 24. Phone 22-20.
Koszalin (c)
Avenue Zwyciestwa 20. Phone 37-57.
Lodz (c)
Avenue Piotrkowska 72. Phone 3-70-77.
Lublin (c)
Avenue Krakowskie Przedmiescie 29. Phone 26-85.
Olsztyn (c)
Avenue Dabrowszczakow 8/9. Phone 23-12.
Plock (c)
Narutowicza Square 1. Phone 29-83.
Poznan (c)
Wolnosci Square 3. Phone 540-11.
Radom (c)
Avenue Zeromskiego 36. Phone 13-82.
Sopot (c)
Avenue Bohaterow Monte Cassino 33. Phone 51-10-39.
Szczecin (c)
Avenue Woj.Polskiego 1. Phone 451-54.
Torun (c)
Avenue Zeglarska 31. Phone 28-72.
Wroclaw (c)
Avenue Swierczewskiego 62. Phone 387-45.
Zakopane (c)
Avenue Kosciuszki 4. Phone 28-12.

PTTK—THE POLISH TOURIST ASSOCIATION

Another recognized organisation with a wide network of offices, many in the smaller towns not served by Orbis, PTTK are able to arrange sightseeing excursions with guides and supply the usual tourist information.

They also run a chain of tourist grade hotels usually

named Dom Wycieczkowy or Dom Turysty. Many are sited in ancient or historic buildings. The accommodation provided is of the simpler kind. For young people on a budget holiday they offer dormitory accommodation.

Their head office is in Warsaw at 124, Marszalkowska Street.

HOTEL ACCOMMODATION

We found little to complain about in Polish hotels. Most offered a very high standard of accommodation, though we thought in a hotel of the standard of the Grand in Warsaw, reputed one of Poland's best, that plugs for the handbasins should have been among essentials. As it was, the piping hot water ran down the open plug hole. It must be admitted that this was the only hotel where we found a lack of plugs, though it did have bathroom clothes lines for drying washing. However as a golf ball fits all sizes of plug holes we always carry one in case of such emergencies.

All the rooms we slept in were comfortably furnished, with plenty of wardrobe space and such essentials as clothes hangers and shoe cleaning materials. The floors invariably had fitted carpets. Though there were room radios we could only tune in to Eastern European stations or Radio Luxembourg. Radio reception was generally poor and after a few unsuccessful attempts to cut out interference we did not bother.

Every hotel had a good restaurant mostly with a western style band playing during the evening dinner meal in case you wanted to dance.

In the main, hotels were clean with plenty of bathroom linen. The bed linen was frequently changed, but we wished the Poles would make up the beds. When you went to get into them you would discover the edges of the bed clothes neatly turned back instead of tucked in which meant bed making when tired. This custom was found throughout Poland. We also discovered the Poles favoured enormously high pillows, with bolsters under the bed head to keep us propped into an almost sitting position. We soon learned to remove them so we could enjoy the luxuriously soft down pillows.

There were always plenty of blankets, with spares at the foot of the bed. Woven to keep out the winter cold they were hot and heavy and we found one to be more than enough.

Hotel accommodation must be purchased in the form of a voucher or exchange order before a visa for your journey will be issued.

These are the main grades of accommodation and the prices quoted are per person to cover full board accommodation for one day.

S. Category denotes superior hotels—usually the leading hotels in Poland with the best furnishings and service as well as high class restaurants and coffee rooms with music provided for diners. The cost of a room with private bath and all meals is $12.50 a day.

First Class Category hotels ensure hot and cold running water in the bedroom, room telephones, good restaurants and coffee rooms and linguists employed among the staff. The price of a room with private bath and all meals is $10 a day.

Second Class Category Hotels are very much simpler. Usually the rooms only have cold running water though the restaurant facilities are normally quite good with quantity compensating for any lack in quality. A room with full board costs around $7.50 a day.

Third Class Category Hotels are very modestly furnished. Found in the smaller cities, it is unlikely that any members of the staff speak a foreign language. Accommodation costs are around $5.60 a day.

Tourist Category Hotels. These are operated by PTTK and classifications are slightly lower than those of normal hotels with prices correspondingly cheaper.

Children between 4 and 12 years normally get a 25 per cent reduction.

If you buy a voucher for hotel accommodation and then find on arrival in Poland that you are staying with friends and are not going to use it, the value will be refunded in Poland at the prevailing exchange rate of 23.95 zlotys to $1.

In Poland hotel rooms are reserved from 6.00 p.m. to 6.00 p.m. the next day, unlike most other parts of Europe where the room has to be vacated at 10.00 a.m.

PENSION AND BUNGALOW ACCOMMODATION

Orbis run a number of family type pensions which provide good but simple accommodation and the opportunity to eat local Polish dishes. They also operate some Bungalow Camps in popular resorts. Apart from Miedzyzdroje, Swinoujscie and Leba where you can book for short periods including a single day, in the main in order to use this cheaper accommodation you must book for a 10 day period preferably beginning on the 1st, 11th or 21st of a month.

Here are some of the places where this type of accommodation is to be found together with the full board costs per person per day.

Miedzyzdroje and Swinoujscie, small seaside resorts in north-west Poland—$5; Zakopane, the popular Tatras mountain resort $3.50–$4.50; Ciechocinek and Krynica, both spa resorts $3.50.

At the Leba holiday village you can book accommodation in a two bedded bungalow for $3.50 a day or in a four bedded bungalow for $3 a day.

CAMPING

Poland with her lakes, mountains, rivers and forests is a camper's paradise. But you cannot camp haphazardly as in most western European countries. You are required to buy camping vouchers with which to pay your costs and to stay at one of the forty camping sites spread across the country, all in wonderful scenic surroundings. Most camping sites operate from the beginning of June until the middle of September.

Provided you have your own camping gear the cost of a camping voucher is $3 per person per day which covers the site charge and the provision of three meals. There are no children's reductions.

Camping vouchers can be bought from Orbis agents in Britain. On arrival in Poland the vouchers are exchanged into Polish currency for you to pay the camp managers as you go along.

It costs from 20 c. to 40 c. a night to stay in one of the site's tents, the same amount if you pitch your own tent, and $1.05 if you would prefer to stay in a hut. The cost for parking a car on the site varies from 40 c. to 50 c. (10–12 zlotys) and the same for a caravan.

If this buying and exchanging of camping vouchers should seem complicated, try to realise that the Poles are anxious to earn foreign currency. By ensuring you pay for camping vouchers before you travel they will know they have accumulated a little more currency to assist them in the rebuilding of Poland.

The Orbis-Polish Travel Office at 313, Regent Street, London, W.1, are able on request to supply you with a list of all Polish camping sites.

FOOD AND DRINK

Before we went we knew little about Polish cooking, but found it surprisingly suited to British palates.

The Poles make sure you will not go hungry. The day starts with a full breakfast of Polish ham covered with slices of cheese, bacon or ham and eggs, eggs boiled, poached, scrambled, served in a tumbler or fried, boiled sausages and plenty of new white rolls, creamy butter and jam including fig jam.

This is washed down by excellent coffee either served black or with milk and cream. Tea—known as herbata —is also widely drunk. Though it arrives without milk, if you ask, milk is quickly forthcoming. The trouble with the tea is the habit of serving it in glass tumblers which are too hot to handle until the tea begins to get cold. However it is reasonably strong and among the best served on the Continent.

Lunch normally consisted of an hors d'oeuvre, followed by soup, a main meat dish and ended with a beautiful cream pastry, ice cream or a compote of fresh fruit. There was little choice of sweet dishes.

Dinner is a similar kind of meal. There are plenty of schnitzels, veal cutlets and steaks, only we discovered the Poles have the habit of mincing steak before cooking so it arrives in the style of a 'hamburger'. If you want something like our definition of steak you must ask for 'steak anglais'. Poultry, especially duck with apple sauce, is also popular.

Among the wide range of soups, beetroot soup accompanied by a small patty was one of our especial favourites.

These are some of the specialities the Poles served to us and which made a welcome change to the international fare of many of the larger hotel restaurants.

Bigos (sauerkraut with meat); Kolduny (dumplings

stuffed with mutton); Golombli (cabbage leaves stuffed with meat); Fried goose served with sauerkraut; Roast hare in a cream sauce with a kind of beetroot purée. We also ate wild mountain strawberries dusted with icing sugar. Then of course there were the well-known Polish smoked meats, ham, loin of pork and sausages of all kinds.

Meal prices were not all that expensive. Here are the prices of some types of dishes served in Orbis restaurants.

		From	*To*	
(a)	Cold snacks	5.00	25.00	zlotys
(b)	Hot snacks	10.00	15.00	
(c)	Soups	3.00	6.00	
(d)	Fish	13.00	30.00	
(e)	Poultry	10.00	30.00	
(f)	Meat	15.00	28.00	
(g)	Desserts	5.00	15.00	

And do try pastries with your afternoon cup of tea. Their chocolate, coffee, almond cakes are delicious but very rich. The gingerbread and honey babas, and the maorkas—pastry filled with dried fruits, almonds and nuts—also took our fancy, so did the cheese cake whose filling was garnished with pieces of fresh apricot. Tea and cakes used to cost about 50 c. for each person which we regarded as surprisingly cheap.

Restaurant service was also surprisingly good after our experiences in other Eastern European countries, and we found in Poland that we could eat a meal quite comfortably in under an hour.

Apart from tea and coffee there is little to drink in Poland. It is not a wine producing country, and wine imported from Rumania, Bulgaria and Yugoslavia costs from 70 to 100 zlotys a bottle (well over $3). The national drink is vodka and though at the start you may not exactly like it, if you persevere you will find it is not so bad after all.

Poland does brew some very good lager beers. Our favourite was 'Okocium O.K.Beer' which cost about 4 zlotys a bottle.

CIGARETTES

Provided you pay in English, American or other foreign currencies, many brands of British and American cigarettes can be bought at 35 c. for a packet of 20. They are stocked at the kiosks in most Orbis hotels. If you fancy trying Polish brands 'Carmen' at 12 zlotys for 20 are the best buy, 'Caro' at 11 zlotys are also a superior brand though most Poles settle for 'Silesia' at 5.20 zlotys a packet.

Needless to say the Poles like British and American cigarettes and we often used to slip a coach driver a packet instead of giving a monetary tip.

WHAT TO WEAR

Though the Poles do not dress up, they are always neatly dressed. Polish women, who because of high clothing costs patronise home dressmakers, wear those clothes with a flair and are among Europe's most elegant women.

If you pack the same type of clothes as you would if visiting a British holiday centre you will not go far wrong.

Our own luggage was not spectacular. I took a lounge suit for the evenings and my wife took one or two smarter summer dresses and we found these suitable for even top grade restaurants and hotels.

In the towns ladies will find a lightweight suit of jersey wool, courtelle or cloth quite handy. If you are going to the Baltic take some beachwear. Bikinis are popular with Polish women and the men's bathing trunks seemed a little scantier than those worn on home beaches. For the mountains, skirts, wool twin-sets and stout walking shoes.

For men the usual sports clothes for day wear and in case you do strike a hot spell a few cricket or beach shirts.

If you are travelling in spring or autumn a lightweight overcoat is an essential item of clothing—and at all times do not forget a plastic mac.

Winter travellers should take their heaviest coats, snow boots if you have them, ear muffs and thick underwear.

Though you are hardly likely to be turned away if you arrive unsuitably dressed for dining in a smart restaurant, it is only courtesy to wear a lounge suit or a smarter dress.

Though we do not consider ourselves snobs, we were rather appalled when dining with friends in Warsaw's leading hotel to see a party of British male tourists enter in open-neck shirts and flannels. They would never have done this if dining out in Britain and it is doubly important that this kind of thing is not done on the Continent where our manners are watched more closely.

TOILETS

Polish toilets are of the pedestal type. They are clean and wholesome, but do take a supply of toilet paper with you. Though all toilets visited—even those at the summit of mountain railways—did have supplies of this necessary commodity, it was coarse and of very poor quality. This extended to private toilets in hotels.

A 25 groszy charge is usually made, this entitling you

to the coarse paper handed out by the women attendants who also look after the male toilets.

Gentlemen's toilets are indicated by a triangle ▽, ladies by a circle O. Where ladies' and gentlemen's toilets are adjacent the triangle is contained inside the circle ⊽. The presence of toilets can also be indicated by a double O – OO, by the words Mejski (Men) or Damski (Women) or Dla Mezczyzn (Men's Toilet) and Dla Kobiet (Women's Toilet).

TAXIS

Poland has plenty of taxis, even in the smallest provincial towns and they are very well patronised. They are far from expensive, charges being 4 zlotys for the first kilometre and 2 zlotys for every additional one. If you travel beyond the town or city boundary then the charge is increased to 4 zlotys for every kilometre travelled.

There was also the standard charge per kilometre payable between the hours of 11.00 p.m. and 5.00 a.m.

Charges are shown on the taxi meter and there was never any attempt to put one over on us. In fact the taxi men did their best to help us in spite of the difficult language barrier and were among the friendliest of Poles.

Though tips are optional, and I am sure there would have been no scowls had I not done so, the taxi men we met were such genuinely nice people that tipping them was a pleasure.

Polish taxis do not cruise. You either have to telephone for one, or wait at a taxi rank.

Taxi ranks are marked with the words 'Postoj Pla Taksowek Osobowych' in white on a blue background set on a post. Even if there is no taxi when you arrive, wait. Any taxi passing and seeing you standing there will immediately stop even if they already have a fare. It is quite usual for those travelling in the same direction, even though strangers, to share a taxi and halve costs.

TIPPING

Throughout our Polish journey we were never once pressed to give a tip as is the case in so many other countries we have visited. When a tip was offered it was readily accepted. In restaurants the usual service charge was added to the bill. This could be 10 or 15 per cent though in smart restaurants with music for dancing it could be as high as 33 per cent—but it was clearly indicated. The usual amount of money given to taxi drivers etc. was between 5.00 and 10.00 zlotys, according to the distance travelled or the extent of the service rendered to us.

THE BARBER AND HAIRDRESSER

Some of the larger hotels have ladies' and gentlemen's hairdressing salons. Even in the very small towns there are hairdressing salons which seem clean and efficient even though they offer nothing much in the way of decor.

Gentlemen will find a shave costs between 5 and 10 zloty, haircutting between 7 and 10 zloty according to the standard of the salon patronised. A ladies' shampoo and set costs between 25 and 40 zloty.

NEWSPAPERS

The only British newspaper we found was the *Daily Worker* though someone did say they had seen an isolated copy of *The Times*. When tired of the type of news offered by the *Daily Worker* we looked for the American *Christian Science Monitor*.

POSTAGE RATES

It would hardly seem necessary to worry about these in view of the quite extraordinary length of time it takes for a letter or postcard to get out of Poland. Greetings cards sent on the first day of our visit did not reach England until five weeks after the date of postage. Mail arriving three weeks after posting can be considered to have done well. If you are only staying for a fortnight it is more than likely that you will arrive home first. The official rates are: postcards: 1 zloty, letters: 2.50 zloty. For airmail services there is a surcharge of 0.90 zloty. Post offices are open from 8.00 a.m. to 8.00 p.m., though in some major cities the main post office is often open day and night.

BUSINESS HOURS

Shops open around 11.00 a.m. and close at 6.00 or 7.00 p.m. Food shops open at 7.00 a.m. and close at 7.00 p.m. On Sundays and holidays shops are closed, though you may sometimes find a food shop open on a Sunday morning—though when this does happen all the shops in the area participate, opening up in strict rotation.

Restaurants and cafés are always open, many not closing until 2.00 or 3.00 a.m.

SHOPPING IN POLAND

(a) Pekao

Pekao is the name given to special kiosks where

purchases can only be made in exchange for a western currency.

These kiosks are usually to be found in hotels patronised by foreign visitors and are stocked with goods imported from the west.

At the Pekao counters you can buy British and American cigarettes, French perfume, wines and spirits and many other luxury items at considerably less than you would pay for the same articles in Britain. They are very much like the 'Duty Free' shops found at international airports.

They also stock articles of clothing like wool or nylon cardigans and sweaters. These for foreign tourists were not good bargains, but much in demand by Poles who had somehow managed to secure western currency notes and could therefore buy these articles at the Pekao kiosk at less cost than in the surrounding shops.

(b) Kiosks

In every town you will find small street kiosks selling all sorts of things including newspapers, magazines, postcards, stamps, single envelopes and sheets of notepaper, simple toys, small souvenirs and such like. Many of these kiosks open at 6.00 a.m. and do not close until late in the evening.

(c) Souvenir Shops

If you are looking for general souvenirs to bring home look for those shops which accept Orbis coupons. This will help to keep costs to the minimum.

For general type souvenirs of carved wood, dressed dolls, attractive raffia and cloth pictures, amber necklaces and brooches try the Cepelia shops. You will find one in most of the towns and cities visited by tourists.

The Desa shops which specialise in antiques are also

designed for tourist trade and widely spread, so are the Jublier chain which trade in metal wear and high class cutlery.

PHOTOGRAPHY

You can use your camera freely in Poland, provided you do not try to take pictures of military, industrial or transport installations. It is also forbidden to take pictures when flying over Poland.

REGISTRATION

A foreign tourist, staying in Poland more than 30 days, must register either at the Foreign Visitors' Registration Office (Biuro Rejestracji Cudzoziemcow) in Warsaw, should this be his first stop in Poland, or at the nearest Voivodship or District (Powiat) Militia Station of the locality where he first stays.

Visitors staying less than 30 days are not required to register with the Police. Normally, civil registration is arranged by hotel reception, hostel or camping site management or persons with whom you will be staying while in Poland.

PUBLIC HOLIDAYS

When it comes to official days off, Poland with its strong religious tradition does better than most Eastern European countries. These are recognised public holidays:

New Year's Day.	January 1st.
Easter Monday.	
Labour Day.	May 1st.
Corpus Christi.	
National Day.	July 22nd.
All Saints' Day.	November 1st.
Christmas.	December 25th and 26th.

5. Zelazowa Wola—the room in which Frederic Chopin was born

6. The Royal Summer Palace at Wilanow, near Warsaw

7. A village wedding
group at Lowicz

8. Old fortifications
at Cracow

CULTURAL ENTERTAINMENT

Theatre, opera, concert and cinema performances usually start at 7.00 or 7.30 p.m. Seats can be booked in advance at any Orbis office.

Seat prices are as follows:

Theatre	8.00 to 30.00 zloty.
Opera	12.00 to 35.00 zloty.
Operetta	10.00 to 35.00 zloty.
Concerts	6.00 to 25.00 zloty.
Cinema	4.00 to 15.00 zloty.

PUBLIC TRANSPORT

Having seen the way people pack themselves into buses, trolleybuses and trams, the latter running through the streets of Warsaw during rush hours so full that people are hanging on the outside unable to get in, if you still wish to turn yourself into a sardine you will find that they have one fare irrespective of the distance travelled. Bus fares 00.80 groszy; trolleybuses 00.60 groszy; trams 00.50 groszy. There is a special night fare between 11.00 p.m. and 5.00 a.m. of 00.90 groszy.

FISHING

Poland, with her lakes running into several thousands not to mention her many rivers and streams is an angler's paradise. Not only can you enjoy fishing surrounded by charming scenery, but you are assured of good sport by the trout, pike, salmon, perch, eels and dace which swarm in these waters.

The Poles have organised their main fishing areas to provide plenty of simple, cheap accommodation in special fishermen's shelters or in private houses. Costs including meals average about $3.85 a day.

An angler's licence with a validity of up to 14 days costs $5. This entitles you to all types of fishing in still or running waters except in the special breeding areas.

If you feel you need a special fishing guide, you can hire one for around $7.25 a day—though with so many fish waiting to be lifted from the waters this would seem a quite unnecessary expense.

Boats can also be hired quite cheaply. A rowing boat for two to three persons costs as little as 85 c. a day, a double canoe 55 c.

HUNTING

Some of the finest hunting grounds in Europe are to be found in Poland's game forests which cover 25 per cent of the country.

From earliest times sportsmen have flocked to Poland to enjoy some rare sport. King Casimir Jagellion enjoyed his hunting so much that he spent seven years of his reign hunting in Poland's forests, his councillors having to travel from Cracow to find him, hoping they could engage his attention so that important state matters could be talked about.

Accounts of some of the spectacular hunts in Poland's forests by European royalty of the nineteenth century can be read about in old books. In our own lifetime the Polish hunting expeditions of Hermann Goering made international headlines.

One would imagine that so much organised slaughter would long ago have decimated Poland's wild animals. But this is not so. According to 1962 statistics, 19,300 wild boars, 10,063 stag, 25,171 roebuck, 24,000 foxes and the unbelievable total of 429,600 hares were shot by hunters in Poland's forests. Perhaps three times as many winged game were taken in the same year.

Yet as we found on our travels, game is still very plentiful and on the main road into Zakopane from Nowy Targ a car ran into a small herd of roebuck crossing the road within inches of our bus, injuring two of them.

Some Polish game, notably the very rare bison, elk and bears, are protected. But that still leaves you wild boar, wolves, lynx, roebuck, fox, badger, grouse, greyhen, partridges, pheasants and varied water birds.

Shooting expeditions for individual travellers are during the following periods arranged by Orbis.

Red deer	21st August to 11th February
Roe does	1st October to 10th February
Roe bucks	20th May to 20th October
Wild boar	1st August to 10th February
Fallow deer	1st October to 10th February
Lynx	1st November to 31st March
Wolves and foxes	All the year round
Woodcock	1st August to 31st May
Wild Duck	1st August to 30th November
Wild Geese	1st August to 30th April
Capercaillie	15th March to 20th May.

If you decide on a shooting holiday, you will have the unforgettable experience of being accommodated in the simple home of a forest game-keeper. Here you will be able to observe the daily routine of Polish country life while enjoying the warm hospitality which will at once make you feel like a friend rather than a paying guest.

Orbis organise special hunts for visitors and have hunting centres in various parts of Poland.

On average the cost of a day's shooting works out at $10.65 per person—but if this price looks high, remember it includes your food and accommodation as well as an interpreter's services.

The London office of Orbis can give you full particulars of organised shooting holidays.

The Language

When you notice for the first time those Polish shop signs, or try to read the Polish newspapers piled for sale in those bright little street kiosks, you will feel that this is a language you will never be able to master. All those joined consonants look quite unintelligible. All those odd nasal vowel sounds. All that hissing and shushing as the Poles chatter in restaurants or on street corners makes it all seem so much more difficult.

No Pole would be rash enough to try to convince you that his was a language easily learned or understood. It is different to all other Slav languages. You can take some comfort in knowing that the position is no easier for Slavs living outside and visiting Poland.

In addition to standard Polish (since the twelfth century the Cracow dialect has been regarded as the purest pronunciation) they are up against six widely spoken regional dialects considered part of the ordinary everyday Polish language.

There is little need to worry about the language. We were surprised by the numbers of Poles who spoke and understood English. Many Poles, especially in the mining areas of Silesia, having for a time worked in French or Belgian pits, speak and understand French. A considerable amount of German is spoken in the Gdansk, Szczecin and Wroclaw regions. Never worry, you will get by as easily as we did.

Like German the Polish language has three genders—masculine, feminine and neuter. Vowels tend to be short and sharp, the last word-syllables accentuated.

This being so, where should we begin or perhaps more important what must you know to get by?

We might as well begin with the vowels.

Letters	*Pronunciation*
a	As in the word ARE
e	*En* as in the word HEN or PEN or DEN
y	As in the word IT
i	Pronounced *ee* as in SEE
o	As in HOT or DOT or SHOT
u and ó	As in LOOT or BOOT or ROOT
ę	As in UN
ą	As in ON

Most of the consonants have the same sound as our own, but it would not be Poland if there were no exceptions.

The letter W tends to be pronounced as a V while the letter C has a sound very much as though someone was sneezing like TCH or TZ as in Tsar. The J also seemed different, sounding like a Y as in the word 'Yeah!'

Then of course there are those mysterious joined consonants which have their own special sounds.

Letters	*Pronunciation*
dz	Is pronounced as it reads.
dź	The accent over the z gives this the sound J
cz	Becomes *ch* as in CHURCH
ch	Is pronounced like the *ch* in the word LOCH
ci	This is confusing as it also sounds like *ch* in LOCH
sz	These are the letters which gives the Polish language its shushing sound.
ź	This sounds like the French word JE
s	Another shushing letter as in SHOP
ł	An odd-looking letter like an l crossed out is actually the Polish w sound as in WAY

Having learned all those strange sounds you will feel confident to have a go yourself. When battling with a fresh and difficult language we usually find a shopping expedition gets us over the first hurdles and unlocks our tongue. In fact we usually start by trying to count our money.

The Polish Numbers

1. Jeden	2. Dwa	3. Trzy
4. Cztery	5. Pieć	6. Zześć
7. Siedem	8. Osiem	9. Dziewiec
10. Dziesięc	11. Jedenascie	15. Pietnascie
20. Dwadzieścia	50. Piedziesiąt	100. Sto
1000. Tysiac		

The Days of the Week

Sunday	Niedziela	Monday	Poniedzialek
Tuesday	Wtorek	Wednesday	Sroda
Thursday	Czwartek	Friday	Piąter
Saturday	Sobota		

Week Tudzien   Month Miesiąc   Year Rok

Months of the Year

January	Styczen	February	Luty
March	Marzec	April	Kwiecien
May	Maj	June	Czerwiec
July	Lipiec	August	Sierpien
September	Wrzesiem	October	Październik
November	Listopad	December	Grudzien

The Day

Today	Dzisiat	Tomorrow	Jutro
Morning	Rano	Noon	Poludnie
Afternoon	Popołudniu	Evening	Wieczór
Night	Nocy		

Some Useful Polish Words and Phrases

Yes Tak		No Nie	I Ja
Please	Proszę	Excuse me	Przepraszam
Thank you	Dziękuję		
Good morning	Dzien Dobry	Good evening	Dobry Wieczór
Good night	Dobranoc	Goodbye	Do Widzenia

Some Useful Words when Shopping

How much?	Ile	Price	Cena
Weigh	Ważyć	Bill	Rachuner
Cheap	Tanio	Colour	Kolor
Dear	Drogo	Enough	Dosyć
Expensive	Kosztowne	Less	Mniej
More	Więcej		

At the Greengrocer's

Fruit	Owoce	Apples	Jabłka
Cherries	Czereśnie	Grapes	Winogrona
Lemon	Łacytryna	Nuts	Orzechy
Orange	Pomarańcz	Pears	Gruszki
Plums	Śliwki	Strawberries	Truskawki

At the Dairy

Milk	Mleko	Butter	Masło
Cheese	Ser	Egg	Jajko
Margarine	Margaryna		

Drinks

Beer	Piwo	Brandy	Koniak
Coffee	Kawa	Glass	Szklanka
Lemonade	Lemoniada	Liqueur	Likier
Mineral Water	Woda Mineralna	Soda Water	Woda Sodowa
Tea	Herbata	Vodka	Wódka
Water	Woda	Wine	Wino

Food

Beef	Wolowina	Beefsteak	Befsztyk
Bread	Chleb	Cake	Ciastko
Chicken	Kurczę	Fish	Ryba
Ham	Szynka	Liver	Watroba
Meat	Mięsco	Mutton	Baranina
Omelette	Omlet	Pork	Wieprzowina
Roast	Pieczony	Sausage	Kielbasa
Soup	Zupa	Veal	Cielęcina

Vegetables

Bean	Fasola	Cabbage	Kapusta
Carrot	Marchew	Green Peas	Groszek Zielony
Potatoes	Ziemniaki	Salad	Salata
Tomatoes	Pomidory	Vegetables	Jarzyny

Miscellaneous Words

Boy	Chłopiec	Brother	Brat
Child	Dziecko	Daughter	Córka
Father	Ojciec	Friend	Przyjaciel
Husband	Mąz	Wife	Zóna
Sister	Siostra		

At the Post Office

Letter	List	Post Office	Poczta
Postcard	Pocztówka	Stamp	Znacziek
Telegram	Depesza		Pocztowy
Telephone	Telephon	Telegraph	Telegraf

At the Bank

Change	Bilon	Currency	Waluta
Bank Note	Banknoty	Coin	Moneta
Cheques	Czeki	Money	Pieniądze

Useful Words When Travelling

Aerodrome	Lotnisko	Aeroplane	Samolot
Airport	Port Lotniczy	Boat	Lódź
Departure	Wyjazd	Harbour	Przystán
Luggage	Bagaź	Platform	Peron
Port	Port	Porter	Bagaźowy
Railway	Kolej	Ship	Statek
Station	Dworzec Kolejowy	Taxi	Taksowka
Ticket	Bilet	Ticket	
Train	Pociąg	Office	Kasa Biletowa

Useful Words For The Motorist

Brake	Hamulec	Carburettor	Gaźnik
Change the Battery	Zmienić Akumulator		
Change the Plug	Zmienić Świecę		
Engine	Motor	Petrol	Stacja
Garage	Garaz	Station	Benzynowa
Oil	Olej	Gear Box	Skrzynka Biegów
Petrol	Benzyna		

A short list, maybe—but a list which will get you by. After all, you will find as we did that it is easier to master an odd word than a complicated phrase, and it is amazing with a courteous, intelligent people like the

72

Poles how quickly they catch on to the odd word and in a flash understand just what you are after.

We find it great fun to try out odd words in a strange language and are delighted when we find that despite our atrocious pronunciation we have made ourselves understood.

PART III

WARSAW—THE MARTYRED CITY

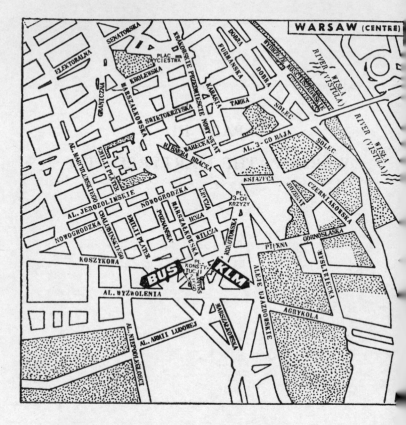

KLM KLM INFORMATION OFFICE
1, Plac Konstytucji,
Warsaw
Telephone: 217041 (after office hours 43112

BUS 9, Warynskiego
Warsaw
Telephone: 217021

Airport: KLM: telephone: 221816

WARSAW—THE MARTYRED CITY

There is no other city in the world quite like Warsaw. The War shattered scores of European cities. None shared Warsaw's fate. Six years of war and as a city Warsaw ceased to exist.

To understand the martyrdom of Warsaw between September 1939 and January 1945, you must know something of Germany's master plan for Poland.

The plan put into action from the moment Poland was over-run was first to kill off every Pole then to incorporate Poland within the boundaries of the 'New Germany', populating the rich Polish countryside with settlers transplanted from the heart of Germany.

Warsaw had hardly been occupied before the massacres began. In five years of German occupation Warsaw's population dwindled from 1,300,000 to 160,000, most of whom had taken refuge in the Praga district on the east side of the Vistula where the German troops were billeted, and because of this did not suffer the wanton destruction as happened to other parts of the city. It is said that from the ruins of the west bank no more than 15 survivors crawled to welcome the liberating Soviet Army marching into the city on the 17th January 1945.

During those long years of occupation Warsaw experienced successive waves of bestial terror and simple heroism. Listening to the Poles talking about those times you feel your flesh beginning to creep, but at the same time you feel proud to know these people who after enduring years of inhuman torment can find sufficient courage to laugh about it.

Tens of thousands of the city's inhabitants were tortured to death in prisons and concentration camps. Warsaw's children were shipped off to Germany never to be heard of again. Mass executions by shooting were commonplace. Gallows disfigured the streets. Starvation and mass deportations were the order of the day.

Yet despite the waves of systematic murder and brute terror, aimed at reducing the city to the size of a provincial town with a proposed all-German population of no more than 200,000, Warsaw resisted. The final blow for freedom was begun on the 1st August 1944 when the citizens of Warsaw struck back at the Germans in a fight which lasted 63 days.

On the west bank of the Vistula the whole city took part in the struggle. Forty-three thousand men were directly engaged in fighting the enemy who after the initial shock of the rising fought back with bombs, tanks and mortars. The weapons of the Poles were no more than 5,000 rifles and pistols supplemented by 25,000 'Molotov Cocktails'.

It says much for Polish toughness and patriotism that this scratch citizens' army could have held out for so long when faced with one of the finest fighting machines in the world. But hold out they did, battling in the streets, in the churches and eventually in the sewers beneath the city, inflicting 25,000 casualties on the Nazis who retaliated by massacring 150,000 of Warsaw's citizens, many of whom were driven alive into the burning buildings.

Though the citizens looked for aid either from the Russians or from the other Allies it did not arrive. The British tried an unsuccessful arms drop. The Red Army who were already on the east bank of the Vistula almost in sight of the city were held by the Germans and though they too tried to drop arms, their planes were intercepted and driven off.

On October 2nd 1944 Warsaw surrendered. The Germans immediately shot the leaders of the rebellion and expelled the entire population, who were marched from the capital, leaving behind no less than 250,000 dead.

Now the Nazis really got to work on Warsaw. With the aid of specially trained units known as the 'vernichtungs' commando or annihilation squads they began by removing all remaining works of art, furniture, museum pieces, manuscripts and other objects of value. When this had been completed special machines were brought into the city to tear up the tramlines, telephone cables, water and electricity mains. They were followed by the flame throwers and dynamite squads who went from street to street and house to house burning and blowing up everything from the humblest worker's cottage to the finest churches and historical monuments.

This was no haphazard destruction. It was methodically planned, lasting for more than three months. The parks did not escape either. Even the trees were uprooted and burned. When the squads finished 85 per cent of the city had been destroyed. This included the total destruction of 11,299 buildings, the partial destruction of 14,269 more, while of the 957 historical buildings in the city almost 800 were no more than shapeless rubble heaps.

Only the arrival in Warsaw on 17th January 1945 of the Soviet Army prevented everything from becoming a rubble heap—but though the shells of some buildings still pointed skywards Warsaw was hardly more than a name given to a heap of scorched bricks concealing a quarter of a million mouldering corpses.

Within days of liberation people began to reappear in the city centre, having crossed from Praga or walked back to Warsaw from the countryside where thousands had hidden themselves. The opening of the work camps and prisons put thousands more people on the snow-covered roads leading back to Warsaw—people prepared to endure further hardship among the rubble while they set about rebuilding the city which had come to mean so much to all of them.

On February 1st 1945 the Polish Government announced that though ruined, Warsaw still remained Poland's capital—a decision welcomed by the entire Polish nation.

The Poles talk with grim amusement about those early days of 1945. Of peasant carts in place of trams and buses, of pedal taxis with people sitting on seats fixed to bicycle handlebars while the cyclists pedalled away behind. Of the hundreds of people killed every week by falling masonry as the severe winter frosts caused gutted buildings to collapse into the streets.

It was a city of black marketeers in which a two-ounce bar of chocolate fetched $2.10, a second-hand bicycle $280. Everyone from cabinet minister to engine driver was happy to accept a standard wage of 300 zloty (then about $2.10) a week plus two free meals a day. Everyone had ration cards which only guaranteed you a ration of anything which might happen to arrive in the city.

Warsaw's troglodytes, in an effort to make a better living in their cellar homes, scavenged among the ruins in the hope of finding something they might be able to sell. When nothing more was to be found small family treasures which had been cherished during the War were disposed of.

Those who had spent months and years in concentration camps sold the clothes they stood up in, somehow surviving without overcoats, socks or underwear the Polish winter of 1945.

When we shook our heads and asked how it was possible to live in such conditions our Polish friends smiled 'You forget we're Poles. Besides it wasn't so bad once we learned to accept it!'

With a steadily growing population prepared to live in such conditions until Warsaw was rebuilt the Government soon got to work. Spacious new industrial and residential districts were planned, parks laid out.

While the plans were being drawn up armies of ordinary men and women toiled with shovels or their bare hands stacking the bricks which might be used for rebuilding and removing the putrefying corpses for decent burial.

This was the start of the 'Warsaw miracle'—a miracle which caused the world to shake its head in disbelief as in less than twenty years a wilderness of rubble became the beautiful flourishing city of more than one million people, which you are now about to visit and enjoy.

You may feel this introduction has been a trifle on the long side, but to appreciate Warsaw you have to appreciate the history of the last thirty years as well, remembering the city you are visiting has been rebuilt almost from scratch with the aid of engravings, photographs and descriptions of the old Warsaw which they have so lovingly re-created, much of it with the old stone. Where new stone has been used it has often been artificially weathered to give it the appearance of age so that it does not destroy the character of the building on which it has been used.

When I say Warsaw is a city which everyone should cherish I really mean it. One of its greatest attractions is the vivacity of its citizens. I was captivated by them, anxious to shake hands with almost every man and woman in sight, knowing that by their willing acceptance of untold hardship coupled with personal self-sacrifice on an unbelievable scale they had made everything I was now seeing and experiencing in Warsaw possible, even if there are still some ugly gaps waiting to be filled.

It is interesting to realise Warsaw is the geographical centre of Europe as well as being almost in the centre of Poland itself.

The River Vistula cuts the city into two parts. Old Warsaw is built on the higher right bank. The Praga district on the left bank is a smart residential area of nine-storeyed apartment blocks, the part known as Praga II reached by crossing the double-tiered Gdansk bridge being the more impressive.

The first thing every visitor to Warsaw does is to have a look at the *Palace of Science and Culture* (*Palace Kultury i Nauki*) which whether you are driving in from the airport or arriving by train is the first thing to catch your eye. Not only does it dominate the vast expanse of the *Parade Square* (*Plac Defilad*) but the whole of Warsaw.

Though in the very heart of their city, most Warsaw citizens regard it without favour. We found it ugly, but oddly impressive.

It was given by the Soviet Union to the Polish Nation, took three years to build and was completed in 1955.

From the ground to the TV mast on its central pinnacle is 722 feet. The pinnacle is surrounded by four towers and if you take the trouble to count as we did, you will find each of these towers is five-storeyed, which gives you some idea of the height of the place, which is rather lost on account of the heavier bulk of the base buildings with their acres of windows and vast doorways shadowed by ornate porticos supported on Corinthian styled columns.

You can go in, entrance being from Marszalkowska Street. The inside is a wonderland of coloured marbles lit by crystal chandeliers and is surprisingly impressive —almost as impressive as the statistics which were trotted out by a patient guide who in half the European languages referred to its 3,300 rooms which accommodated up to 12,000 people while the Congress Chamber, one of Europe's largest, can seat 3,000 more. Hidden away in its vastness we found two theatres—one on each side of the entrance hall—two cinemas, a museum, a Palace of Youth as well as a sizable swimming pool and several educational institutes. Full of people coming and going and long crocodiles of tourists it was like a busy little self-contained city.

We took the lift from the entrance hall and were shot to the 30th floor and went out on to the wide terrace for an unforgettable view of Warsaw.

It is quite easy to pick out the new thoroughfares and the residential areas with their vast apartment blocks. But your attention will be drawn to the old city with huddled roofs which, still looking a bit too new, can do with a bit of weathering. You can also pick out the fragments of the town walls with the fine old barbican, with the Vistula and Praga providing a contrasting backdrop.

It's great fun standing high above the city looking at the faces of the trippers as they first step on to the terrace to stare over the city to the green and gold countryside beyond. Some are obviously frightened at being at such a great height and stand well back from the parapet. Others make your hair rise as they peer downwards to the streets immediately below. You will find an hour spent inside the Palace of Science and Culture is far from being wasted.

Like most capital cities Warsaw has so much to offer

that those with limited time have to decide what really is worth seeing and what can be safely omitted.

We began our sightseeing from the *Plac Zamkowy* or Castle Square. In the centre stands the tall slender column with the statue of King Sigismund III on top. There is little that is impressive about this place, it being like the market square of any large provincial town with its friendly three and four-storeyed buildings with steep red roofs.

The Sigismund Column is the oldest as well as the best loved of Warsaw's monuments. Put up in 1644 it received the 'full treatment' by the Nazi annihilation squads who set their tanks against it, shattering the column into hundreds of pieces. Though damaged the statue of the king escaped destruction. The column was re-erected in 1949 overlooking all that is left of the former *Royal Palace* built between the fourteenth and eighteenth centuries. Sacked, bombed and dynamited by the Nazis in 1944 it was completely destroyed.

However before it was sacked the Polish Resistance had been active and under the very noses of the Nazis had managed to remove some of its furnishings. Some fragments of the interior were sorted from the ruins to be used in the reconstruction.

Slightly below the Royal Palace—it is built on a slightly higher level—you will see the baroque *Palac Pod Blacha*. Though this was burnt in 1924, when Warsaw was rebuilding after the War it was decided to include this building too.

Behind Plac Zamkowy and reached along Piwna and Swietojanska Streets (have a look at the *Church of St. Martin* with its lovely courtyard) is the *Stare Miasto* or Old Town which grew up in the fourteenth century on the site of an older settlement of wood and wattle behind solid ramparts.

84

Before the last War this was a densely populated warren of beautiful yet decaying dwellings, mostly of the seventeenth and eighteenth centuries, surrounded by a ring of defence walls.

During the 1944 rising this densely populated labyrinth was for the patriots a natural defence area and was fortified in the best way possible. As a result this quarter of the city not only saw some of its fiercest fighting but after air attacks, continuous bombardments by German artillery and tanks and searing by the flame-throwers it was reduced to heaps of stones and ashes covering thousands of bodies.

When the Town Planning Council asked the people who had returned to the shattered city what they considered should be the first priority in the rebuilding programme then being drawn up, the majority vote was for the Old Town which also contained the Cathedral of St. John (Katedra Sw. Jana) built between the fourteenth and sixteenth centuries and also destroyed in the 1944 fighting.

It would have been easy enough to reconstruct the area you are now visiting, throwing up a series of distinctive modern buildings very similar to those you see across the river in Praga, above its favourable Vistula site. To have done so would have defied the Polish love for tradition. It was tradition as much as the desire to provide future generations with an idea of Poland's cultural heritage which made the planners rebuild the Old Town to look as it was before the first German bombs fell on it in September 1939.

Photographs, engravings and scattered archives were examined. Where a description of a house or monument was known to be in existence it was read and studied by architects and stone-masons who then set about re-creating the work of those sixteenth century builders who first fashioned this lovely corner of the city.

The result of their labours is remarkable especially around the *Old Town Square—Rynek Starego Miasta—* which with its re-created Renaissance and baroque houses coloured in rich shades of ochre, gold and green is still Warsaw's loveliest spot.

The original buildings were the homes of noblemen and rich merchants whose status could be gauged by the number of windows and the intricacy of the designs on the house fronts.

Though full of beauty, this corner of Warsaw has lost much of its original character. Perhaps it is too spick and span. Maybe there are too many tourists wandering the narrow cobbled streets, taking photographs of the Rynek or viewing the sweep of the Vistula from Celna Street. As a work of painstaking reconstruction it is of course remarkable. To judge what has been accomplished not only here but throughout Warsaw, start off as we did by seeing the twenty-minute film pieced together from German newsreels of the destruction of Warsaw. It is shown without charge to visitors at the Warsaw City Historical Museum in the north-west corner of the Rynek, a dark stone building on a corner site where Nowomiejska Street runs into the square.

Many of the old houses claim special attention. Number 27 the 'Winiarnia Fukiera' is a four-hundred-year-old wine shop with an attractive courtyard. Something of a show place, it is one of the few places in Warsaw where you can get a good glass of wine. Popular with tourists and citizens alike, we found it on the lively side.

Number 29 belonged to the influential Giza family. Following the death of his beautiful wife, King Sigismund August was so upset that his nobles were afraid he would go mad. They therefore consulted Twardowski, a Polish sorcerer of the time, making him promise to help the king, a promise Twardowski kept. He knew very well what would happen if he refused.

Having persuaded the king the ghost of his dead wife would appear, he substituted for the ghost the beautiful Basia Gizanka who so charmed the king that he forgot his dead wife and fell in love with Basia, which improved the Giza family's fortune.

The oldest house is Number 31. It has some reconstructed fifteenth century Gothic work, a lovely seventeenth century oriel with a sixteenth century statue of St. Anne in a niche.

The houses on the north-west side have been taken over to form the *Warsaw City Historical Museum*. We found this well worth seeing not only for its strangely moving film of Warsaw's destruction, but for its diagrams and many prints showing Warsaw's turbulent history.

Number 32 must surely be the most beautiful house in the Old Town. Number 36 has a fine ornamented front with a sculpted Negro's head which was the trade mark of the seventeenth century owners.

Houses Nos. 18 to 20 form the *Adam Mickiewicz Museum*. Adam Mickiewicz (1798–1855) was Poland's most famous poet, as well as a dramatist, publicist, and politician who having spent most of his adult life in exile died in Istanbul while trying to raise a Polish Liberation Army. His body now rests with other Polish heroes in Cracow's Wawel Cathedral.

Some of the least important houses on the Rynek have been turned into restaurants and coffee houses. When you are looking through the windows at the passing tourists as you wait for the next course to arrive, you might care to remember that in the square stood the pillory in which so many Polish patriots found themselves standing side by side with common felons who on such occasions found themselves very gently treated.

Have a look at the *Cathedral of St. John*, which is to be found in Swietojanska Street. Most citizens will tell you they prefer to worship there and on Sundays it is always full. Built at the beginning of the fourteenth century, in 1944 during the Warsaw Rising it was the scene of some of the bitterest and bloodiest fighting. When the insurrection was over the Germans took their revenge. The ruins were dynamited and what was left was burned to the ground.

Before reconstruction the heaps of stones were lovingly turned over and any fragments worth preserving were rescued and incorporated in the new building which was restored in its original Gothic style. In the side chapel dedicated to the Baryczka family there is a fine sixteenth century Spanish crucifix reputed to be miraculous. We were told that in the sixteenth century the hair on the statue used to grow and was only cut once a year by a girl chosen from the Warsaw virgins. When and why the hair stopped growing we were not able to discover—but having examined the statue closely we could find no indication of it ever having been hirsute. The only other item of real interest is the sixteenth century tomb of one of the Dukes of Mazovia which is to be seen in the choir.

In the cathedral crypt there are several tombs including those of several Archbishops of Warsaw, that of Gabriel Narutowicz, a Polish President who died in 1922, and Henryk Sienkiewicz whose novel *Quo Vadis* was awarded the Nobel Prize for literature in 1905 and has been twice filmed.

Leave the cathedral by the side door on the right-hand side. This takes you into Dzienka Street beneath the arcades which used to connect the cathedral with the

Royal Castle. In these arcades an attempt was made on the life of King Sigismund who was only saved by the prompt action of his son. You are now in Kanonia Street whose beautiful baroque houses have been carefully restored. It was here that the Canons of the cathedral lived.

Kanonia Street leads you back to the Rynek by way of Celna Street. Leave the Rynek by way of Nowomiejska Street if you want to see the *Barbican* and the other mediaeval fortifications rebuilt from fragments of the original walls dug from the rubble. The double row of ramparts are protected by the remains of a moat and by the Barbican with cone-shaped towers and strong-looking battlements under which you walk on your way to the Nowe Miasto or New Town.

Though the reconstructed Barbican is going to interest you and your camera—practically everyone seemed to stop to take a snap—you are just as likely to pause to look at some of the paintings so often exhibited here by Warsaw's young avant-garde painters who have found the background of the old red brick walls a perfect setting for the somewhat startling paintings they delight in showing.

Our guide explained the name *Nowe Miasto* or *New Town* was something of a misnomer as the town was here before the fifteenth century and was quite autonomous with its own municipal authorities. Like the Old Town it saw some of the worst street fighting of 1944 and was left in ruins by the Germans. Reconstructed after the liberation, most of the buildings were rebuilt in the graceful styles of the seventeenth and eighteenth centuries.

Begin in Freta Street into which Nowomiejska Street has led you. Walking north you pass the rebuilt churches of *St. Paul* (also known as the Holy Ghost Church) and the *Church of St. James* as well as the *Dominican Monastery* whose reconstruction was made possible by money provided by Polish Americans.

In 1867 Marie Sklodowska was born in *Number 16 Freta Street*. Married, and as Madame Curie, she became an outstanding chemist and physicist receiving the Nobel Prize in 1903 and 1911 for her work on and with radium. There is a plaque on the house wall so you are not likely to miss it. The second plaque recalls the death here of the leaders of the 1944 Warsaw Rising. Beneath the plaque you will see wreaths and flowers of remembrance. Everywhere in Warsaw where groups of patriots died or were executed by the Germans you will see small plaques and beneath them wreaths and bunches of flowers which when they begin to fade are at once renewed by the ordinary people who keep faith with those who died in the struggle for liberty.

Freta Street leads you to the *Rynek Novomiejski* or *New Market* dominated by the domed *Church of the Sisters of the Blessed Sacrament* built by King John Sobieski III in 1683 to commemorate his victory over the Turks at Vienna.

The Rynek Nowomiejski is very quiet—just a backwater of the city. I am certain that, apart from the church, if the guide had not made a special point of drawing our attention to its former importance we would hardly have noticed it. Those walking around Warsaw might care to remember that here you will find both a ladies' and gentlemen's toilet.

Close by is the *Church of the Blessed Virgin Mary*. Built in the fourteenth century on high ground overlooking the Vistula, it is the oldest of Warsaw's many churches. Its belfry is the most impressive in the city.

Continue along Koscielna and Franciszkanska Streets to the start of Anielewicza Avenue, named after the young Jewish leader of the 1943 Ghetto Rising. Take one of the turnings on your right into Lewartowski Street. You are now in the new Muranow residential district built on the site of the *Warsaw Ghetto*.

Before the war 30 per cent of Warsaw's population were Jews. Some assimilated into the Polish population. The majority however clung to Jewish tradition, caftans, curls and beards stamping the menfolk and lending to this corner of Warsaw colour and character. Today in this part of the city there is not one beard or caftan to be seen.

Since they first settled in Poland during the fourteenth century at the invitation of Casimir the Great there is a wonderful history of peaceful co-existence between the Poles and the Jews.

The anti-Semitism which momentarily surfaced in the nineteenth century was largely due to Russian influence. The Tsar had decreed that Russia's Jews must live in the outer provinces. As Poland was counted a Russian province it was natural that the Jews should choose to settle there rather than go east into the cold wastes of Siberia.

When Poland was invaded in 1939 it was estimated that her Jewish population was in the region of $3\frac{1}{2}$ to 4 millions, the largest in the world outside the United States of America.

Anti-Semitism, so often a product of jealousy of Jewish wealth and achievement, never became a Polish problem when the poverty of the Polish Jew out-matched that of the Polish peasant which was miserable enough.

But a life of poverty meant nothing to the Nazis bent on the 'Final Solution' to the Jewish question. Every Jew coming under Nazi conquest was automatically sentenced to death.

By early 1940 Poland's Jews were being rounded up

by the Nazis and herded back to the Ghettos. Living fifteen to twenty to a room with little food and poor sanitary arrangements thousands conveniently died of disease and starvation, though for Nazi comfort far too many continued to survive these inhuman living conditions.

The younger, stronger Jews were sterilised before being sent to forced labour camps to work until they died from a mixture of malnutrition and exhaustion. Thousands were massacred in the first primitive extermination chambers set up in the back of army lorries. It was not until 1942 that Auschwitz had really turned mass murder into a flourishing industry.

By 1942 the Jews knew they were all living on borrowed time. The Polish Resistance did everything they could to help those herded into the ghettos, smuggling in food and a limited amount of arms.

As early as 1941 the Germans had surrounded Warsaw's ghetto by a high wall, Jews only being marched out to become forced labourers in nearby industrial plants or to be marched to the trains which had already started their tragic journeys to the ovens and gas chambers of Auschwitz.

But like the Masda Jews who when surrounded by the Roman legions fought back and in the end preferred death to capture, the Jews packed into Warsaw's ghetto became equally determined to put up a fight and to die fighting.

On the 19th April 1943—Easter Monday—the Poles heard rapid gunfire behind the ghetto walls. The fighting had started.

Everyone in Warsaw, Poles, Germans and Jews, knew the rising must fail. Hemmed in behind the restraining walls with every house packed tight with women, children and old men with little food and hardly any ammunition, these superbly brave but doomed people spurred on by Mordechai Anielewicza battled magnificently but hopelessly against German tanks, artillery and flame-throwers while bombs rained down on their houses.

For almost a month the Jews fought against these impossible odds until on 16th May Mordechai Anielewicza with twenty companions was consumed by flame-throwers as they made a last stand in a small bunker.

The last shot fired, the Nazis moved into the ghetto blowing up and burning the houses, killing or deporting those Jews who had somehow managed to survive the month of battle.

The ghetto rising ended in Zamenhoff Street. Today it is a large grassy space surrounded by new apartment buildings, many with open air kindergartens where children can be seen playing on swings, see-saws and in the sandpits with tiny flower gardens around them.

Yet somehow it seems that the whole area revolves around the simple and not overlarge monument commemorating the heroes of the ghetto. A granite prism-like block of blackish stone designed by the sculptor Nathan Rappaport has two bronze bas-reliefs. On one a group of young Jews are shown fighting. On the other women and old men are depicted leaving the ghetto. Looking across the open space its simplicity was impressive.

It is terribly ironic to realise that the stone from which it was fashioned was originally intended by the Germans as the base for a monument to Hitler.

On looking at the new apartment houses, you will realise some are built on a slightly higher level. So thoroughly had the Germans carried out their work of destruction that it was quite impossible to shift the accumulated mountain of rubble, which in places was levelled off and the new housing blocks built on top of it.

Close by these raised houses is all that is left of the notorious *Gesiowka Prison* used during the occupation by the Gestapo. The Poles are now working on the remains of the building before opening it as a museum.

In front of its gates is a small tree, its trunk covered with black-edged memorial cards giving the names of those who died here. In a patch of earth under the tree, is a simple wooden wartime memorial cross covering the grave of one martyr as well as the customary wreath and bunches of remembrance flowers.

Having explored this area return to Anielewicza Street and left into Marcelego Nowotoki Street which although lined with apartment houses does because of some open spaces levelled and grass-grown seem oddly unfinished. This is one of the oddities of Warsaw. One minute you seem to be in a long complete street which suddenly opens up into a flat grass-grown open space leaving you wondering whether this is part of the new city plan or a spot yet to be built over.

On your right going south you will pass the reconstructed *Mostowski Palace* facing the seventeenth century *Arsenal*. Before reaching *Felix Dziezwinski Square* which though not very big is one of the most satisfying dominated by the old colonnaded buildings of the *Ministry of Finance* and the *Bank of Poland*, go to Number 79 Swierczewiskiego Avenue which is almost on the corner where in the *Jewish Historical Institute* you will find a permanent exhibition on the rising in the Warsaw ghetto and which only too vividly enables you to relive the events of those terrible days. This is something you should see.

Walk along the *Senatorska* in the heart of Warsaw's new residential district and you will come to the *Plac Teatralny* or Theatre Square with tall office buildings and the beautiful *Teatr Wieiki*—Grand Theatre—which seating two thousand people is Poland's largest theatre.

In its right wing you will find the *Polish National Theatre*. If you enjoy opera and ballet at its colourful best, this is the place to make for during your stay in Warsaw.

Built after the design of an Italian architect Antonio Corazzi between 1825 and 1833, it was burned down in 1939, reconstructed in 1949 and with its up to date stage equipment and lighting claims to be one of Europe's outstanding theatres. If you do decide to go inside, spare time to have a look at the *Theatrical Museum*. We found it most interesting.

The *Monument to the Heroes of Warsaw* is in the centre of Theatre Square and you are not likely to miss it. It commemorates those who died in the city during the war. It is in the form of a simple plinth topped by a bronze mermaid—the emblem of Warsaw. The simple inscription 'To the Heroes of Warsaw 1939–1945' somehow seems just right. There is no need to describe their heroism. It is too well-known.

Looking around the Plac Teatralny our first impressions were not altogether favourable, with the monumental classical architecture of Corazzi's Grand Theatre seeming to clash with the simple monument to the Heroes of Warsaw and the tall office blocks with ground floor shops which have already been built on the east side of the square.

However as you get used to this odd mixture of old and new, you find it has all been well thought-out and for us the final impression of Theatre Square was remarkably satisfying.

Leaving Theatre Square by the Senatorska walk towards your starting point the Plac Zamkowy. On your right is the *Palac Prymaskowski* which belonged to the powerful Polish primates. Built in the seventeenth and eighteenth centuries in a pleasing horse-shoe shape, it was rebuilt after the war. Though Poland still has a primate, the palace has been taken over as offices by the Ministry of Culture.

If you have followed our route so far, you will have seen many of the most interesting corners of Warsaw, but a visit to the city will remain incomplete without a walk along the *Krakowskie Przedmiescie* and *Nowy Swiat* which together form the two and a half mile 'Royal Road'. Stretching from the Plac Zamkowy to the Plac Trzech Krzyzy and lined with churches, palaces, shops, restaurants, cafés, tea rooms and offices they are by far the most interesting streets in Warsaw.

Of all the reconstructed areas, the *Krakowskie Przedmiescie* seemed to have worked out the best, not because the work on the buildings had been done so well, but because the entire street was so redolent of the atmosphere of the eighteenth century. Though buses and cars passed by and there are always plenty of people to be seen on the pavements, there is an impression of leisured old-world elegance.

Maybe it is because no tall modern buildings disfigure its low skyline, or perhaps its collection of eighteenth century churches and palaces are packed so tightly as to create the impression of another age, or maybe the many trees and the small flower beds in the palace courtyards have something to do with it.

Whatever it is, we loved to wander along this beautiful historic thoroughfare, finding it far more satisfying than the bustling modern boulevards in other parts of the city.

Start from Plac Zamkowy leaving the Sigismund column behind you. On your left is the *Mariesztat* giving a fine view of the five mile east-west thoroughfare

9. Cracow—the cathedral on the Wawel Hill

10. Cracow—the Royal Castle on the Wawel Hill

11. St. Mary's Church, Cracow

12. Nidzica Castle above the Dunajec River

linking the Praga area across the Vistula with the city centre.

At the very beginning of the Krakowskie Przedmiescie, the *Church of St. Anne* is worth looking at. It has a fine rococo choir, some excellent eighteenth century woodcarving and Gothic vaulting.

Next door, in the grey arcaded building, Madame Curie carried out her very first experiments.

The street now widens into a tiny square with neat lawns, flowers and a scattering of spruce and willow trees. At the centre is the statue of the poet and patriot Adam Mickiewicz. Destroyed in the war, it was subsequently recast. In the small coffee house opposite, Chopin who lived in this street used to sit in his younger days.

The baroque *Church of the Carmelites* escaped wartime destruction. Built in the eighteenth century, it should not be missed as it conveys the original beauty of the Warsaw churches.

Next door is the *Radziwill Palace*. Built during the seventeenth and eighteenth centuries, it has beautiful wrought iron gates, lawns and flowers and a small ornamental pond. It is now the meeting place of the Polish Council of Ministers. Opposite is the *Potocki Palace*, one of the loveliest in Warsaw, where Napoleon courted Marie Walewska. The palace is now used as an office block by the Ministry of Art and Culture.

The rather old-fashioned tourist hotels Bristol and Europejski overlook the *Plac Zwyciestwy* (Victory Square) where Napoleon and other generals have reviewed their victorious troops.

The *Saxon Gardens* (Ogrod Saski) laid out in 1727 by King August II of Saxony, though part of the Royal Palace, became Poland's first public park.

Little remains of the eighteenth century palace apart

from a portion of the arcades. Under a metal plate below this squat, three-arched fragment with its balustrade and the shattered bases of the columns which formed the original portico, are the remains of Poland's unknown soldier.

Chosen from the many who died in the heroic defence of the town of Lwow, as the defenders included old men, women and boys, whether these remains are those of a male or female, old or young is a matter for conjecture. But does it really matter all that much—sufficient that whoever it is died in defence of Poland. In the urns mounted on the stone blocks is earth from those Second World War battlefields on which Polish troops fought and died. On the stones are the names of the battles fought. Guarded by soldiers in long black coats with rifles slung loosely over their shoulders, we thought this one of the most moving memorials we had seen anywhere.

The baroque eighteenth century *Church of the Order of Visitation* (even more of a mouthful when spelt out in Polish) has a beautiful front which caught our attention, even though next door in what used to be the *Tyszkiewicz and Uhruski Palaces* is part of Warsaw's famous university.

Immediately opposite is the *Czapski Palace* where at one time Chopin's parents lived. They were only employed in the role of higher paid servants. It was from the Czapski Palace that Chopin left Poland in 1830. We thought it somehow appropriate that today the palace should be the home of the Polish Academy of Fine Arts.

The *Church of the Holy Cross* can easily be distinguished by the great stone figure of Christ bowed down by his cross. This church was the scene of some terrible fighting during the rising of 1944, the battle raging inside the church which was severely damaged. Its main interest is the side pillar in the left aisle where sealed in an urn is the heart of Frederick Chopin, removed from his body before it was buried in the Père Lachaise cemetery in Paris. You are not likely to have to search for the pillar which is usually surrounded by sightseers though there's little enough to see.

The Krakowskie Przedmiescie ends at the *Staszic Palace*, an ugly nineteenth century building now the Polish Academy of Science. The seated statue in front of the building is of Nicolaus Copernicus the medieval astronomer and prelate born at Torun in Western Poland in 1473. He was the first man to put forward the theory of the earth revolving around the sun—a theory taken up later by Galileo and Sir Isaac Newton. The statue you see was the work of the famous Danish sculptor Bertel Thorwaldsen and was erected in 1830.

If the day chosen to explore this part of Warsaw happens to be hot call in at Number 52 where they serve excellent wine.

Nowy Swiat or New World Street is a continuation of the Krakowskie Przedmiescie. It is the busiest and best loved street in the city and we found it among the liveliest after dark with some good restaurants and cabarets and places where you can dance.

If you are a lover of Chopin, take a walk down Ordynacka Street which is half-way down Nowy Swiat on the left-hand side and you will get to the *Ostrogski Palace* which has been turned into the Frederick Chopin Institute with all kinds of bric-a-brac connected with Chopin's life and work.

There is a very colourful legend attached to the palace and the guides make certain that tourists are given the fullest particulars. It would seem that in the days of once-upon-a-time in the palace cellars there was a lake hiding a vast treasure guarded by a golden duck. The duck gave a soldier who happened to find the lake a bag of gold telling him that if he spent the money wisely there would be more where that came from.

True to fairy tale tradition the soldier squandered the gold on a good time. Asked by a beggar for money to buy food the soldier gave him the lowliest coin in his pocket.

When the bag of gold had been spent the soldier went back for more only to find the duck and the lake had vanished never to be seen by any living soul again.

On the left-hand corner of Nowy Swiat and Jerozolimskie (Jerusalem) Avenue you will see the vast modern building of the Central Committee of the Polish United Workers' Party. Built of light sandstone around an inner courtyard it is one of the most impressive of Warsaw's new style buildings though with its severe lines not to everybody's taste.

If you turn down Jerozolimskie Avenue and keep on the same side of the road as the vast building you will reach Poland's *National Museum*. Not only is this the largest museum in Poland with almost one hundred exhibition rooms, but a museum full of good things very well arranged.

Old masters of the Dutch, Italian, French and German schools of painting contrast with contemporary Russian and Polish art and Picasso ceramics. A cold wet day in Warsaw is quickly forgotten inside the National Museum.

Should you manage to exhaust its treasures and find you have time to spare, call in next door at the *Polish Army Museum* which is an eye-opener on Poland's endless fight for freedom and also has on display some frightful-looking weapons designed to do a bloody job with cold efficiency.

The Nowy Swiat ends in the *Plac Trzech Krzyzy*

(Square of the Three Crosses) which got its name from three columns each topped by a gilt cross which were erected in the eighteenth century to mark the start of this pilgrims' road.

In the centre of the square is the *Church of St. Alexander*. If you think you recognise it take heart. It is a replica of the Pantheon in Rome. Built in the early nineteenth century during the 'romantic period' it was almost totally destroyed by the Nazis in 1944 but has been rebuilt.

On the right in the car park you will find horse-drawn fiacres for hire and close by behind the privets ladies' and gentlemen's toilets.

Beyond the Plac Trzech Krzyzy is the lovely *Ujazdowskie Avenue* with some important-looking buildings—mostly Embassies—the *Polish Parliament House* which is open to visitors though we did not visit it and the *Ujazdowskie* and *Lazienki Parks* and *Botanical Gardens* which must be seen.

Sunday is the best day for a walk down Ujazdowskie Avenue—that is when the people congregate from all parts of Warsaw to enjoy the sunshine, eat ice cream and cakes in open air cafés, or gather around the odd, rather impressionist *Chopin Monument* set on high ground overlooking the lake in the Lazienki Park.

This is a replica of the original monument. Though a romantic composer Chopin has had a remarkable effect on Polish life, his music fanning Polish patriotism during partition. Taking no chances of Chopin's statue becoming a resistance symbol, in 1940 the Nazis blew it up.

Recast in 1958 by the resilient Poles, the statue is now back in place and considered one of the city sights.

Lazienki Park is Warsaw's equivalent to London's Hyde Park or New York's Central Park. However, we thought it was very much more than just another open space for a big city. In fact it is an eighteenth century landscape garden which has been preserved with very few changes.

Going in through the fine wrought-iron gate, take the path between the high banks. This will lead you to the eighteenth century *Orangery* which has a small royal theatre inside. The impressive equestrian statue in front of the building is a copy of the statue of Prince Josef Poniatowski by Thorwaldsen, a Danish sculptor. Blown up by the Nazis, the new statue was a gift to Warsaw from the city of Copenhagen.

The *Bialy Domek* or White Cottage built in 1774 in which King Stanislaw Augustus lived while the palace was being built is close by. At one time it was a home from home for the future Louis XVIII of France who lived in it during a period of exile.

Set on an island and framed by trees seen across the lake, the *Lazienki Palace* looks every inch the royal palace of fairy tales. With a graceful portico and terrace leading down to the lake it really is quite lovely. It does not take much imagination to see why the Poles consider it the finest eighteenth century palace in the country.

Designed by an Italian—Domenico Merlin—some of Poland's finest eighteenth century artists and sculptors decorated it outside and in. At one time a fine collection of paintings hung in the picture gallery but in 1944 the retreating Nazis carried away all the paintings and furniture before setting the palace alight. They had made plans to dynamite the walls but had insufficient time though they had bored no less than four hundred holes in the structure in which to pack the explosive charges.

Rebuilt after the war, the palace picture gallery which

can be visited was rehung with some good paintings including a Breughel and though it conveys some of the splendour of the original you are somehow left with the feeling that what you are now looking at is second-hand.

On leaving the palace cross the lake bridge. Have a quick look at the open air *Teatr Na Wyspie* (Island Theatre) which was built in 1790 and is a copy of the Roman theatre at Herculaneum. The stage with its classical ruins and stone busts of the world's great dramatists, Shakespeare included, is to say the least unusual.

Having seen all there is to see in and around the palace make your way back to Ujadowskie Avenue and take a short walk up Bagateza Street to *Plac Unii Lubelskiej* where you will find one of Warsaw's very largest supermarkets. The Poles have not been slow to adopt this western staff-saving shopping idea. Even though not wanting to buy anything, it is always fun to wander around to see what is for sale and what the housewives are buying. This vast supermarket is never short of free-spending customers.

Now turn north into *Marszalkowska Street* and walk in the direction of the Palace of Culture. It is one of the longest and widest of Warsaw's main streets. On its left side building has more or less been completed with an almost continual row of well designed seven-storeyed apartment blocks with large shops at street level.

Cut in half by the enormous Plac Defilad with the huge Palace of Science and Culture, its continuation towards the Saski Gardens is marred by a collection of tiny, neat, prefabricated shops mostly selling clothes, though one did have a good display of Polish crystal.

Much of the right-hand side of the street is still in the builders' hands—but when finished the tall cube-shaped apartment blocks and some of the more fancifully

103

designed commercial buildings, especially the Polish Bank's circular steel, glass, concrete and chrome office which is being put up opposite the Palace of Science and Culture will make that particular building less of an eyesore.

The Polish excursion guides make a point of ignoring the great Russian-inspired building, imagining people in their coach won't see it and ask questions about it, though its very size makes such an idea ludicrous.

Some people feel this attitude towards the building is political. Others claim the dislike to be based on the fact that it is out of keeping with the new city which has been designed. Whatever the real reason the Poles certainly try their hardest to forget it is there.

Arrived back at the Palace of Science and Culture you will most certainly have seen all Warsaw's conventional sights.

But you will never really get to know a city if you stick to its museums and monuments, you must study the people.

We started off by hiring a lovely old horse-drawn fiacre which we found in the rank in the Trzech Krzyzy Square. Our driver was a veritable patriarch with a weather-beaten face and twinkling blue eyes above a heavy grey moustache. He certainly had a way with horses. He coaxed his beast with a click of the tongue and a few quiet words spoken in the sibilant language of the Poles which sounds like the hiss of escaping gas.

Poles tell you they have almost as many horses as cars and far too many hours are spent keeping the beasts spruce and shining. Looking at this sleek well-groomed horse we were prepared to believe everything we had been told about their love of horses and for that matter all animals.

A fiacre's slow pace gives you plenty of time to study

the people in the street without their ever becoming aware that you are staring at them.

The Poles are smart dressers. We saw plenty of teen-agers but even though some girls did wear slacks they were beautifully groomed with tidy hair. We do not remember seeing one youngster with that brand of grubbiness which marks so many of our own young people.

You will certainly want to go to the cinema. Polish films are excellent with a certain bitter-sweet quality which we find endearing. Polish film makers are now turning out sophisticated comedies with much of the realism toned down by whiffs of sheer fantasy which reflects something of the Polish character, the Poles themselves being romantic realists.

There are more than seventy cinemas in Warsaw, many with wide screens. We saw French, Italian, American and British films advertised and were told they normally did capacity business. This is due to the Polish fixation about life in the west. It is rather sad that they equate the day to day happenings of the cinema screen with the kind of life you and I lead.

Poles are also fond of the theatre. Warsaw has more than twenty theatres—a remarkable number for a city still in the process of being rebuilt. We did not visit any of them. We felt sure that the subtle nuances of the plays would be lost to us due to the impossible language barrier. A Canadian woman married to an emigré Pole and familiar with the Polish language saw a historical play and spoke enthusiastically about the staging, costumes and lighting which she claimed to be equal to any she had seen in London and New York. Even Warsaw's children have their own theatre.

The people of Warsaw love good music and crowd the concerts at the National Philharmonic Hall, the Opera and the special Operetta Theatre. Poland has no less than nine State Symphony Orchestras and ten Philharmonic Societies, so during your holiday you have more than an even chance of listening to at least one of them.

Because the Poles like good music do not dismiss them as a nation of 'squares'. Plenty of Warsaw clubs and restaurants have excellent dance bands. Poles know how to dance the twist just as well as you and no matter what dance the bands played, there was never a shortage of couples on the dance floor. Polish people dance a great deal. An evening of dancing in a restaurant is often topped off with a visit to one of the young people's clubs which flourish all over the city, or to the Stodola (the Barn) a huge hall where youngsters gather to dance or enjoy traditional type jazz. You may even end in a stark cellar where smoochy music, smoke and one or two vodkas make the whole place oddly erotic. In fact during our stay in Warsaw we often arrived back at the hotel with the dawn.

Sometimes we patronised the 'Praha' self-service restaurant on the right-hand side of Jerozolimskie Avenue, between Krucza Street and Nowy Swiat opposite the Central Departmental Store. It claims to serve upwards of 15,000 meals a day. The food always tasted good and prices were low.

As you wander the streets you can still see plenty of signs of Poland's wartime agony. Among the new buildings you might notice an old house of dusty red brick pitted by bullets and shrapnel, or you may see courtyard walls blackened by fire.

We found Warsaw to be a most interesting city. There is certainly plenty to see and do, and though we will be the first to admit it might not be everyone's 'cup of tea' when it comes to holidays we feel it deserves far more than the two or three days most travellers put aside to 'do' Warsaw.

INFORMATION FOR THOSE PLANNING TO STAY IN WARSAW

(1) *How to Reach Warsaw*

There are direct flights by BEA, LOT (Polish Airlines) and AEROFLOT (Russian Airlines) from London to Warsaw. Airlines offering transfer flights to Warsaw include Air France, Czechoslovakian Airlines, KLM, SABENA, S.A.S. and Swissair.

Travellers by rail will find through trains to Warsaw from Ostend and also from the Hook of Holland.

(2) *Hotels*

In S (Luxury) category. Grand Orbis (623 beds) Krucza. 28. Phone 2109. Orbis Bristol (334 beds) Krakowskie Przedmiescie 42/43. Telephone 26-32-41. Europejski Orbis (416 beds) Krakowskie Przedmiescie 13. Telephone 26-50-51.

In 1st Class category.
Hotel MDM (221 beds) Konstytucji Square 1. Telephone 21-62-11.
Hotel Polonia (365 beds) Jerozolimskie Avenue 45. Telephone 28-34-61.
Hotel Warszawa (391 beds) Powstancow Warszawy Square 9. Telephone 26-94-21.
Hotel Saki (140 beds) Zabia 9. Telephone 30-46-11.
Hotel Dom Chlopa (574 beds) Powstancow Warszawy Square 2. Telephone 26-52-61.
Hotel Terminus (70 beds) Rutkowskiego Avenue 28. Telephone 26-95-05.

In 2nd Class category.
Hotel Central (298 beds) Jerozolimskie Avenue 35. Telephone 28-43-07.

Hotel Syrena (285 beds) Gorczewska 28. Telephone 32-12-57.

Hotel Nowa Praga (324 beds) Brechta 7. Telephone 98-234.

In PTTK Tourist Category.

Hotel Dom Turysty (367 beds) Krakowskie Przedmiescie 4/6. Telephone 26-30-11.

(3) *Restaurants*

Warsaw is proud of its restaurants which cater for all tastes and purses. In all the large hotels you will find restaurants, bars and cafés. If you wish to eat in a good class restaurant you will have to reckon on 40–65 zlotys without drinks. But you will find you get good value for the money spent and there is often music, dancing and a cabaret show thrown in. Some restaurants are open to the early hours of the morning—the Poles being 'night birds'.

Here is a short list of some of the more popular places.

Kongresowa—in the Palace of Culture (dancing and cabaret).

Gastronomia. Avenue Smolna 15. (dancing).

Rycerska. Szeroki Dunaj 9/14.

Krokodyl. Rynek Starego Miasta 19/23. (dancing).

Arkady. Marszalkowska 45 (dancing).

Pod Bazyliszkiem. Rynek Starego Miasta 1/9.

Rarytas. Marszalkowska 15 (dancing).

Kameralna. Fukstal 15 (dancing).

Melodia. Nowy Swiat 3/5.

Magnolia. Grojecka 42.

In addition to the above restaurants, there are several which specialise in foreign cooking including the:

Amico. Kredylowa 6. (Jewish dishes).

Balaton. General Zajaczeks 8. (Hungarian dishes).

Samson. Freta 3. (Jewish dishes).
Szanghai. Marszalkowska 53/57. (Chinese dishes).
Trojka—Palace of Culture (Russian dishes).

Those whose budget is limited will find excellent self-service restaurants offering low priced meals. Two we tried were the:
Praha. Jerozolimskie Avenue 11/19.
Frykas. Pulawska Avenue 2. (You will need to look for this one in the big Supersam Supermarket).

(4) *Cafés*

The Poles love café life, so you can expect to find pleasant cafés in all parts of the city, though some of the decor is a bit fanciful. Here are some we tried:
Nowy Swiat. Nowy Swiat 61. (dancing and cabaret).
Pod Gwiazdami. Marszalkowska.85. (dancing).
Largactil. Rynek Starego Miasta 2. (dancing and cabaret).
Alhambra. Jerozolimskie Avenue 32.
Bombonierka. Nowe Miasto 13/15.
Krokodyl. Rynek Starego Miasta 19/23.

(5) *Tea Rooms*

Those who fancy a cup of tea and one of those gorgeous Polish pastries make for Gong, Jerozolimskie Avenue 44. They make a passably good cup of English tea, or if you would like to try Russian tea from a samovar you can get it here too.

(6) *Walking Around Warsaw*

Warsaw's streets are numbered from south to north working inwards from the River Vistula.

You will find plenty of pedestrian crossings indicated by white parallel lines. As the main boulevards are wide and there are tram lines in the centre, take care.

(7) *Trams and Trolleybuses*

Warsaw is well served by trams and trolleybuses. You pay a standard price for your ticket irrespective of the distance to be travelled. This amounts to 50 groszy for a tram ticket and 60 groszy on the trolleybuses. If you use them after 11.00 p.m. you will find the fares doubled.

Rush hour in Poland is different to our own time. The traffic is at its heaviest between 7.00 a.m. and 9.00 a.m. and between 3.00 p.m. and 5.00 p.m. Avoid using public transport during those periods.

(8) *Taxis*

The distinctive white band makes Polish taxis easily recognisable. However, they do not cruise looking for fares, but wait to be called from their ranks which are near the main hotels and at fixed points throughout the city. At the present time (1966) the controlled charge is 4 zlotys for the first kilometre and 2 zlotys for each additional kilometre. Between the hours of 11.00 p.m. and 5.00 a.m. the charge is doubled. The taxis have meters and though Warsaw's taximen are less rapacious than those found in most capital cities, it is as well to check the meter when getting in and out of the cab. Though tips are optional and you will not get a black look if you fail to add a little extra to the fare, tips are welcomed.

(9) *Horse Cabs*

Do try a ride in one of these. They are great fun. You will find horse cabs waiting for customers in the Rynek Starego Miasta (Old Town Square), in the Trzech Krzyzy Square and outside the Central Railway Station. The average charge is 65 zlotys an hour—but the usual custom, provided you can make yourself understood, is to haggle with the driver for a fixed fare covering the

110

length of time you wish to use the fiacre.

(10) *Warsaw's Museums*

Warsaw has seventeen museums which are open daily (except Mondays and on days following a holiday). A small entrance fee is usually charged (about 3 zlotys). The museums in most cases are well worth visiting.

(*a*) *Adam Mickiewicz Museum*. Rynek Starego Miasta 20. Devoted to the life and works of the great Polish poet and political leader.

(*b*) *Museum of the Polish Revolutionary Movement*. Dzierzynski Square 1. A permanent exhibition dealing with the growth of Polish communism.

(*c*) *Warsaw History Museum*. Rynek Starego Miasta 28. Deals with the growth of the city from earliest times.

(*d*) *National Museum*. Jerozolimskie Avenue 3. This combination of Poland's equivalent to our British Museum and National Gallery is a must.

(*e*) *Museum of Culture and Folk Art*. Mlociny 108. For those who like folksy things.

(*f*) *The Lenin Museum*. Swierczewski Avenue 62. If you have visited Lenin Museums in other parts of Eastern Europe, you have also seen this one which is on familiar lines.

(*g*) *Museum of the Polish Army*. Jerozolimskie Avenue 3/5. This was one of our favourites. We found it remarkably interesting.

(*h*) *Archaeology Museum*. Dluga Street 52.

(*i*) *Land Museum*. Ma.Skapie Avenue 20/26. Seemed to deal with Polish agriculture.

(*j*) *Museum of Engineering*. Palace of Science and Culture. For anyone with a hankering after machines.

(*k*) *Theatre Museum*. Moliere Street 2/19. Like all museums dealing with the stage, we found this quite

111

absorbing.

(*l*) *The Jewish Museum* (Jewish Institute). Swierczewski Street 79. Do not miss this museum which tells the story o the Warsaw Ghetto.

(*m*) *Museum of Sport*. Rozbrat Street 26.

(*n*) *Museum of Hunting*. Nowy Swiat 35.

(*o*) *Museum of Culture*. Pulawska Street.

(*p*) *Chopin Museum*. Ostrogoski Palace. Okolnik Street 1. Full of mementos of the life and work of the great Polish composer.

(*q*) *Curie Museum*. Freta Street 16. Entirely devoted to the work of the great Polish scientist Marie Curie-Sklodowskiej.

(11) *Warsaw's Theatres*

The Polish language being difficult to understand, you may feel a visit to a Warsaw theatre is more than you can take. These are the more notable theatres of the city.

Ateneum. Jaracza Street 20.

Dramatyczny. Palace of Culture.

Klasyczny. Palace of Culture.

Narodowny. Teatralny Square 3.

Polski. Karasia Street 2.

Wspotczesny. Mokotowska Street 13.

Zydowski. Krolewska Street 13.

(12) *Children's Theatres*

Known as Lalka, these are to be found in the Palace of Culture and also in the Orangery in the Lazienki Park. In spite of the language barrier these seem more interesting. If you cannot understand what is being said you can watch the faces of the children. And how they do love their special shows.

112

(13) *Satirical Theatre*

It is a great pity that the Polish language is such a barrier, for these satirical theatres are very much a part of Polish everyday life and were 'en vogue' long before TWTWTW made satire fashionable. Many of these lively, witty reviews are performed by students and if you feel you would like to sample one try the Syrena at Litewska Street, 3 or the Komedia Zoliborz at Sierpecka Street 7.

(14) *Cinemas*

The Poles are great film-goers, so you have plenty of cinemas to choose from. These are the most important with the very latest Polish or foreign films to be seen.
Atlantic. Rutkowskiego Street 33.
Bajka. Marszalkowska Street 136.
Luna. Marszalkowska Street 28.
Moskwa. Polawska Street 19.
Skarpa. Kopernika Street 5.
Slask. 3–7, Zurawia Street.
Sala Kongresowa. Palace of Culture.

(15) *Opera*

There are nightly opera performances at Nowogrodzka Street 49.

(16) *Musical Comedy*

Those who enjoy light music will find operetta and musical comedy performances at Pulawska Street 37/39.

(17) *Musical Concerts*

There are usually Friday concerts at the National Philharmonic Hall, Jasna Street 5.

(18) *Horse Racing*

Try to take in a meeting at the Sluzewiec Race Course. It is quite easy to get to. If you do not wish to travel by taxi, the Number 'W' bus from Unia Lubelska Square will take you there. The racing season lasts from May to November and meetings generally take place on Wednesdays, Saturdays and Sundays and on Public Holidays. Entrance costs are from 6–30 zlotys. Poles love race-going just as much as we do.

(19) *Sports Fans*

A visit to the 10th Anniversary Stadium (Stadion Dziesieciolecia) is another must. This magnificent stadium is on the Praga side of the Vistula, and accommodating 100,000 spectators is one of Europe's finest sports arenas. Those occupying the higher tiers, which were built from the rubble of the battered old city, get a splendid view of the city across the broad sweep of the river. During the summer season you can usually find athletic meetings or football matches taking place in the stadium.

Ice skating can be enjoyed at the artificial ice rink Torwar in Czerniakowska Street, while boxing enthusiasts (the Poles are among the world's finest boxers) will usually find a contest taking place at the Gwardia Sports Club in Zelazna Brama Square.

(20) *Theatre, Cinema and Sports Tickets*

Theatre, cinema, opera and tickets for the main sporting events can always be booked in advance at the Orbis office at 16, Bracka Street, or at the theatre booking office at Spatif, 25, Jerozolimskie Avenue.

A theatre or opera ticket will cost you from 10–40 zlotys, but for the cinema 20 zlotys is the ceiling price.

(21) *Car Hire*

Self-drive or chauffeur-driven cars may be hired from the Orbis office, Krakowskie Prezedmiescie 13 (Telephone 26-16-68). A self-drive car costs about $6.50 a day with a 7 c. a kilometre extra charge. For a 4-seater chauffeur-driven Wolga the cost works out at $1.05 an hour plus 10 c. a kilometre.

(22) *Currency Exchange Offices in Warsaw*

Travellers' cheques can be changed at the foreign exchange desks at any of Warsaw's Orbis hotels, at the Central Railway Station, at the Orbis office at 13, Krakowskie Przedmiescie Street; 16, Bracka Street; Konstytucji Square 4.

The Narodowy Bank Polski (National Bank of Poland) at Jasna Street 5 also deals with foreign exchange.

(23) *Post and Telegraph Offices*

The General Post Office at Swietokrzyska Street 31/33 is open day and night. Other post offices are open from 08.00 a.m. to 8.00 p.m. Telegraph offices are open from 7.00 a.m. to 9.00 p.m.

(24) *Excursions*

Excursions in and around Warsaw are organised by Orbis Foreign Tourist Service Office, 13, Karkowskie Przedmiescie Street (Telephone 26-16-68) or by Polskie Towarzystowo Turystyczno—Krajoznawcze (PTTK) Marszalkowska Street 124 (Telephone 60-529).

Pleasure steamers run trips on the River Vistula. They leave from the landing stage on the Wybrzeze Kosciuszkowskie between the Most Slgsko Dabrowski and the Most Poniatowskiego bridges. In addition to the short trips lasting up to 2 hours, you can travel by river steamer to Plock (121 kms.), Wloclawek (167 kms.), Torun (223 kms.), Gdansk (448 kms.).

PART IV
AROUND WARSAW

AROUND WARSAW

There are plenty of places worth visiting around Warsaw. Using local transport some trips can be made quite easily, others on organised excursions. If you are travelling by car it is possible to cover several places in one day.

WILANOW PALACE

Wilanow is only five miles from Warsaw with good tram and bus connections. Warsaw is already beginning to spread southwards, its Sandyba district creeping towards Wilanow. In a few years this lovely spot will be very much part of the city of Warsaw. Already the city considers it—and quite rightly—one of its major show places.

On your way out to Wilanow spend a few minutes at the *Church of St. Boniface* in Czerniakowska Street. One of the few Warsaw churches to have escaped war damage, it was built in the seventeenth century. Frescoes, stucco decoration, paintings and a sixteenth century Dutch triptych make it worth looking at.

With its sentinel poplars on either side, the Daccia Krolewska, or Royal Road, seemed to us the perfect approach to this beautiful baroque palace which some claim to be Poland's most beautiful baroque building.

The construction of Wilanow Palace was started at the end of the seventeenth century. Having become the hero of Europe by beating the Turks at the Battle of Vienna, King John Sobieski III gathered together a group of master builders and architects including a

119

celebrated Italian Agostino Lecci and told them to build him, on the site of an old manor house, a palace to be proud of. The result was Wilanow.

Only the central part of the Sobieski Palace remains. The wings and towers were eighteenth century additions, the palace by then having been sold by Sobieski's son to the wife of one of his hetmen. This energetic woman extended the park and decorated it with statues and had new frescoes painted on the ceilings and walls inside the palace.

The nineteenth century also brought changes, some of the apartments getting a neo-classic face lift, the gardens landscaped and dotted with fanciful pavilions, one in the shape of a Chinese pagoda.

So Wilanow has come down to us with little subsequent alteration apart from the loss of most of the pavilions and of the paintings from the fine picture gallery assembled over a period of 200 years by the owners and which, together with a beautiful collection of period furniture and antiques, were looted by the Nazis and never wholly recovered.

Used by the Nazis as barracks, the palace though shamefully damaged was spared during the destruction of Warsaw, though its few remaining treasures were carried off to Germany.

Lovely at any time, Wilanow is especially attractive in the autumn when the browns and golds of the changing leaves make the dazzling whiteness of the palace façade seem brighter.

Built in two storeys, the front of the palace has ornamental columns and bas-reliefs crowned by an openwork balustrade topped by stone statues. Above the central window there is a copper sun, its metal rays reflecting the sunshine. Copper also covers the cupolas which cap the palace's squat towers.

Wherever you look are statues and mouldings representing the Sobieski coat of arms and his victory at Vienna.

Having looked at the exterior, join a group of tourists waiting to see inside, which with its wall and ceiling paintings, period furniture, antiques is quite wonderful.

The multi-lingual guides, as they take you through the palace which has been restored in a truly masterful fashion, re-create the splendours of eighteenth and nineteenth century Poland with its beautiful women and gallant men who between romances set afoot intrigues directed against the partitioning powers who had split their fine country to fragments.

You will find that Poland's National Museum has restocked Wilanow with portraits of the Sobieski family, paintings and valuable furniture.

Though most tourists are content to spend a few hours at Wilanow you need a half-day to see it properly. If you wish to include the park and gardens a full day is not too long.

ZELAZOWA WOLA—Birthplace of Frederick Chopin.

It is only 35 miles by road from Warsaw to Zelazowa Wola. Though there is a local bus service you should join one of the summer Sunday coach excursions organised by Orbis or PTTK if you wish to enjoy Chopin recitals given by Poland's best pianists.

There's little to see on the journey which follows the main Warsaw–Poznan road through some of Poland's less exciting scenery though, after the main road is left behind, for the last mile or two the scenery is pleasant enough.

Having seen the birthplaces of many writers, musicians and artists, we usually approach further specimens with some misgiving. We were certainly prepared to be disappointed with Zelazowa Wola, but we had reckoned without the Polish talent for painstaking restoration.

We were at once charmed by the tiny one-storeyed cottage shaded by chestnut trees and covered in Virginia creeper, set in a beautiful park of flowers and exotic trees and shrubs given as a tribute to the great Polish composer by the world's Botanical Gardens.

In this tiny house which was the annexe to a long vanished manor house Frederick Chopin was born on February 22nd 1810. At that time his father was tutor to the Skarbeck family who owned the property. Though when less than a year old Chopin moved with his family to Warsaw, he spent many holidays at Zelazowa Wola, his music reflecting the moods of the surrounding countryside as well as peasant tunes of the district. His last visit was in August 1830 just before he left Poland for ever.

The cottage has had a chequered history and when in 1929 it was bought for the Polish nation it was in a sad state. Hardly had the work of reconstruction been completed and the house filled with Chopin relics than the Nazis occupied Poland.

An army unit stationed in the cottage did a great deal of damage, most of the Chopin relics being looted or destroyed.

Reconstruction started in 1947 and is now complete. Furnished with a set of period furniture and a few of the original pictures which had been saved, Zelazowa Wola not only looks like a typical early nineteenth century country cottage, but has an atmosphere which you can almost feel. You seem to anticipate the swirl of crinolines as the Chopin family ghosts pass through the cottage.

On entering turn right into the kitchen. It has lovely hand-painted ceiling beams, an open stove where meals were cooked and a copy of Chopin's portrait by Delacroix; the original is in the Louvre in Paris.

The kitchen leads to the music salon which with white walls, muslin curtains, period furniture and a Steinway grand piano has a touch of real elegance. From this room the Sunday piano recitals are given, while the audiences crowd the outside terraces and spill down the steps into the gardens.

A small cabinet has a plaster cast of Chopin's left hand moulded by Auguste Clesinger, son-in-law of Georges Sand the French woman novelist with whom Chopin had his celebrated romance. In the same case are facsimiles of two of Chopin's early works.

You now pass to the family dining-room with three authentic Canaletto engravings of old Warsaw. The ancient grandfather clock is a real collector's piece and worth looking at.

Crossing the passage you enter his mother's beautifully laid out room. On the walls are copies of family portraits; the originals were destroyed in 1939. The portrait of Chopin's sister Isabella is worth noting. Herself a talented musician, it was Isabella who after Chopin's death brought his heart back to the Poland he loved so much.

On an easel draped in scarlet brocade is a portrait of Chopin. A show case has facsimiles of Chopin's parents' marriage certificate, and his birth certificate. The originals are in the Parish Church at Brochow some five miles away.

The strange-looking musical instrument is known as a giraffe on account of its tall harp-shaped back. Popular in the nineteenth century, it was the type of instrument Chopin's mother would have played, his father accompanying her on his violin. Both parents were fine musicians.

In the alcove dominated by a large white urn which throughout the year is filled with garden flowers, Chopin is thought to have been born.

Now pass into the nursery with its tiny chairs, the greeting cards which the young Chopin sent to his parents and a most beautiful antique inlaid white marble faced wall clock given to the cottage by the present members of the Skarbeck family.

There is little in the father's room, which leads you back to the cottage entrance.

In less than half an hour it is possible to walk around the cottage and to closely examine all the exhibits. But if, like us, you are fortunate to have a sunny day you will retain a vivid memory of light due to white walls lit by sunshine blazing through the large muslin-draped windows, while the simple flower arrangements in every room gives a splash of gay colour. It seems odd that so small a place should have so much period atmosphere.

Spend some time walking in the park with its trees, shrubs, flowers, lake and stream. The work of Francis Kryzywada-Polkowski, it is beautifully laid out.

A visit to the Chopin house, a seat on the terrace for a recital, a walk in the park and lunch in the pavilion restaurant opposite the park gates is a most pleasant way to spend a Polish Sunday.

Advance information about Zelazowa Wola's Chopin recitals can be obtained from the Frederick Chopin Society, Okolnik 1, Warsaw.

NIEBOROW PALACE

From Zelazowa Wola we took the road into Sochaczew then turned south to Bolimow and west to Nieborow, the journey by car taking under half an hour.

The road led past the entrance to the palace which is

a very fine building designed in the seventeenth century for one of the Cardinal Archbishops of Poland by Tylman van Gameren, a fashionable Dutch architect working in Poland at that period, who had a hand at designing many of the more noteworthy palaces dotted across Poland.

After passing into the hands of many famous Polish families, in 1774 Nieborow Palace was sold to Prince Michael Radziwill whose wife Helena Przezdziecki filled it with valuable antiques.

The palace stayed in the hands of the Radziwill family until 1945 when it was acquired by the State and together with the nearby park of Arkadia became part of the National Museum.

Though much of the interior does at the moment look dilapidated, reconstruction is in hand. Even so, we found much to admire in the palace.

The approach is down a short drive and from the door you pass into the entrance hall which has some interesting collectors' items. One of the best of them is a sixth century Roman sculpture of the head of Niobe done in white marble.

Other parts of the Roman collection are in the left-hand corridor which contains busts, tomb stones, urns and sarcophagi.

Our guide told us Henryk Sienkiewicz, author of *Quo Vadis*, based the character of Lydia in his book on an idea got from reading an inscription on one of the tombs which quite simply says 'Marc Vincius. To his very dear wife.'

Reading these words, you wonder what Marc Vincius might have said had he known this stone would one day be carried off to a distant land to become inspiration for one of the finest Polish books ever written, which gained the Nobel Prize for Literature and world-wide recognition for its talented author.

Though the main staircase is by no means grand, the walls and ceiling are covered by hundreds of blue and white Delft tiles put there when the palace was built. Oil paintings help to relieve what to us seemed a somewhat monotonous decoration—the big picture above the curve of the staircase being of King Stanislaw August Poniatowski (1731–1818).

So far only one of the first floor rooms has been completely restored—this being the Green Study. The other rooms, still awaiting attention, do by comparison seem slightly moth-eaten, the silks and brocades used for wall furnishings faded and frayed with age. Even so you can get a very good idea of the splendour of the palace in the eighteenth and nineteenth centuries, the Red Drawing Room with its walls and furniture covered with red and silver matching damask being particularly eye-catching. So too is the room's large portrait of Anna Orzelska (1683–1757) a famous eighteenth century beauty who ended up with a string of children.

In the Yellow Study—you are hardly likely to miss it, the walls being covered with eighteenth century silk in yellow and white stripes with a floral motif—is a strange glass harmonica which looks as though a series of graduated glass dishes have been pushed into one another to form a long horn. Made in the eighteenth century, Mozart, Haydn and Beethoven composed music for it. You may like to hazard a guess as to how it was played and what it sounded like. Our guide had no idea. In the same room the Meissen china chandelier is rather beautiful.

If you are interested in antiques and old portraits, Nieborow Palace has plenty to offer. But do spare a little time to enjoy the lovely palace garden laid out in the eighteenth century after a plan drawn up by the indefatigable Tylman van Gameren.

ARKADIA

From Nieborow continue westwards along the Lowicz road and you will soon come to the romantic Arkadia gardens—a popular excursion from nearby Lowicz as well as from Warsaw.

The garden was laid out in 1778 by Princess Helena Przezdziecka who copied current fashion which demanded that gardens must be landscaped with a lake, pavilions and fanciful trees and shrubs.

In spite of vicissitudes including a little war damage the park has emerged virtually unscathed.

It is quite pleasant to walk in the park, to see the pavilions especially the Temple of Diana which was built on the lake side. With its columned portico, small dome, frescoed interior the work of Jan Piotr Norblin a noted Polish artist of the period, it is quite lovely.

The building known as the 'House of the Arch Priest' has decorations which were carried there from one of the side chapels of Lowicz collegiate church. Another called the 'House of the Margrave' has a reproduction Greek arch close by. The 'Gothic House' has an arcaded gallery and there's an exotic grotto known as Jaskinia Sybilli or Sybil's Den.

To us it all seemed rather strange though oddly attractive, recalling the romanticism and frivolities of the eighteenth century which from France spread across Europe to be cut short eventually by the French Revolution which this type of expensive nonsense did so much to bring about.

Hardly had we left Arkadia at the end of our visit than we were running into the town of Lowicz which is only two miles away.

LOWICZ

Lowicz in the heart of one of Poland's more interesting if less beautiful corners is 55 miles south-west of Warsaw. Its interest is dependent on the local peasantry who in spite of being close to the great cities of Warsaw and Lodz have clung to their costumes, culture and traditions.

The costumes worn on saints' days and Sundays are quite outstanding. In their gaily coloured striped over-skirts which are made of a type of velour, with tight black bodices and white blouses the women look like gay butterflies. Though the young girls are content to wear their hair in plaits or covered with a gay neckerchief some older women prefer the distinctive tall headdress with its long multi-coloured ribbons.

Not so colourful as their wives, the men wear bright coloured baggy trousers tucked into soft black leather Russian type boots. The wide sleeves of their white shirts are caught at the wrist by black heavily embroidered cuffs, the black over-jerkins piped with red are held together with gold buttons and a cummerbund. A group of men and girls packed into a horse-drawn fiacre on their way to a village wedding are a gorgeous sight.

The small village of Zlakow Kosciezny is the show place. Although many women wear local costume to church on Sundays, to see it at its best you should go there at the feast of Corpus Christi when the entire village wearing these wonderful costumes walks from the church in procession through the village.

But for the peasants colour goes further than their costumes. It is also echoed in their house, which although somewhat colourless outside, unless painted deep blue to contrast with the thatched roofs, are inside a riot of rich colours.

If you wish to see inside a typical peasant house, you

3. Rafting down the Dunajec. The author is third from the left in the second row

Tourist Hostel in the Gasiennicowa Valley in the Tatras mountains

15. Peasant costume
in the Tatras
mountains

16. On a road through
the Tatras in
springtime

should take the track to the right opposite the large church of Zlakow Kosciezny. Continue along it for about two miles to the tiny village of Zlakow Borowy. On reaching the village take the left-hand fork and continue until you almost reach the end of the village where you will on your right see a blue-painted cottage with a thatched roof and signposted 'Ceplia'. This is the home of Justyna Grzegora and her crippled husband and you arc invited to visit it.

Entering the cottage we found that it had an earthen floor and a typical hooded stove. Pasted to all the ceiling beams were gay paper cut-outs, these being made by cutting out elaborate designs in coloured paper which are then fixed to a white backing sheet and stuck or pinned to ceiling beams and walls. So beautifully and skilfully are these cut-outs done that unless you look at them carefully you imagine them to be colour prints. All round the living room are brightly painted religious pictures, in one corner a small altar with a crucifix and bouquets of paper flowers. From the ceiling hung an elaborate chandelier made of coloured paper. On the bed were stacked rows of huge embroidered cushions. The hope chest in which valuables and their local costumes were stored was brightly painted, so were the bowls and plates on the dresser. We had seen nothing like it.

But the wonders of the cottage had not ended. When we looked at the earthen floor more closely we found it covered in an elaborate pattern made by pouring sand over the floor. We were invited to have coffee and while it was being prepared we were shown the local costume which was taken from the hope chest.

We realised for the first time that much of the embroidery was not done in silk or wool as we had imagined, but in tiny glass beads. We were also startled by the weight of the costume. We judged the weight of the embroidered apron alone to be at least 2 lb.

We spent some time in Lowicz itself which has a population of around 20,000. Badly damaged during the war, its ancient monuments including the lovely collegiate *Church of St. Mary and St. Nicholas* with its three naves and five side chapels were spared.

In the church are two beautiful tombs, one in marble and the other in alabaster. In them are buried two archbishops. Let into the altar of one side chapel is the fourth century tombstone of St. Victor pilfered from the catacombs in Rome and brought to Lowicz sometime in the sixteenth century. In the church treasury are valuable pictures, sculptures, altar cloths and gold plate. Outside the church, surrounding the extraordinary large market place are some fine houses of the sixteenth–eighteenth centuries.

Most day-trippers visit Lowicz to see its wonderful *Regional Museum* housed in a seventeenth century baroque palace facing the church. This is one place you should not miss, especially the top floor. Here you can see the full range of local costumes including those worn on wedding days. In addition there are glorious paper chandeliers, magnificent paper cut-outs, painted Easter eggs and a whole range of folk art.

This was certainly one of the most colourful museums seen in Poland and worth the journey to Lowicz to see, especially when combined with a visit to the nearby village of Zlakow Kosciezny.

Should you wish to stay for a day or two at Lowicz while exploring the surrounding countryside, the town does have a small hotel—the Miejski (3rd category). We had a meal in the hotel restaurant. Though it was far from the best meal we had in Poland, when it came to quantity we had never seen anything quite like it.

Before we had eaten the first course we were quite full and this was followed by three more. The cost? Under $1.40 a head.

THE KAMPINOS FOREST AND PALMIRY

Though there are bus services to the Kampinos Forest some twelve miles west of Warsaw in the direction of Zelazowa Wola, we did the journey by car.

Warsaw is fortunate in having these 50,000 acres of heath and forest on her doorstep. Forming one of Poland's National Parks it will for all time remain quite unspoiled.

Some time in the past the River Vistula having changed course, the former valley sprouted woods of pine and alder and these with stretches of marshland and sand dunes, some almost 100 feet high, form the Kampinos National Park.

To see the forest at its best make for the village of Sierakow by bus or car, and then take a walk in the forest. At first the stillness may seem oppressive but you grow used to it and readily appreciate the strange beauty of the place.

If you are lucky you may see some wild life, the forest harbouring stags and deer. Should you hear a wild boar rooting in the undergrowth you would be wise to creep away without seeing him, as they can be vicious animals.

Close to Sierakowe in the direction of Pociecha is the nature reservation of Giechowa which has been largely set aside for breeding elk, one time native to the forest.

Starting in 1949 with five elk, they bred so well that by 1956 there were sufficient in the herd to loose some into the forest. You can visit the elk before turning northwards towards the Vistula which quickly brings you to Palmiry.

The day chosen for our forest visit was damp and grey, with a little moisture dripping from the trees, but on reaching Palmiry we realised this was the right atmosphere for the place.

The Nazi plan for annihilation demanded that those whose reputation might make them a rallying point for patriotic demonstrations should be killed. In 1940 the plan was put into operation.

Using forced and doomed labour, the Nazis dug enormous ditches at the edge of the forest before the lorries began to arrive from nearby Warsaw with writers, artists, politicians, actors, sports stars, anyone whom they felt might be a potential danger. Many were accompanied by their wives and children. Among them was Maciej Rataj, President of the Polish Parliament, and Janusz Kusocinski who won a gold medal for the 3,000 metres in the 1937 Berlin Olympics.

In the forest these people were lined up along the edge of the ditches and shot. In one week 2,000 Polish elite died here. When the job had been completed the ditches were filled in and pines planted in an effort to hide the massacre.

After the war the ditches were opened, the bodies exhumed and buried decently.

The inscription at the entrance to the cemetery reads 'It is easy to talk of Poland. More difficult to work for Poland. Harder still to die for her. But hardest of all is to suffer for her.'

Those tragic words were found after the war scratched on the walls of a cell in Warsaw's Gestapo headquarters.

During your Polish journey you will see many reminders of Nazi beastliness, but none will seem quite so poignant as the cemetery at Palmiry especially if you visit it on a dank autumn day.

LODZ

Do not make a special journey to Lodz. Although geographically it is in the centre of Poland and an important industrial city, there is little to see.

Before the early nineteenth century when textile factories were opened with workers imported from Prussia to weave the cloth, it was no more than a small village. By the beginning of the twentieth century Lodz had become Poland's principal textile centre. In 1939 it had a population of around 700,000. Today, Lodz with a population of 723,000 is after Warsaw Poland's largest city with nearly 400 factories.

The only thing worth looking at is the *Art Museum* at 36 Wieckowskiego Avenue which has a good collection of abstract paintings.

LECZYCA AND TUM

Twenty miles north of Lodz is Leczyca with the town walls, moats and citadel erected in the fourteenth century by Casimir the Great. It is old and we found it interesting to walk around.

A mile westwards we discovered the oddly named township of Tum with a history going back to pre-historic times. To the south west of the town you can still see the site of a *fortified pre-historic camp* as well as traces of a *twelfth century stronghold* overlooking the narrow Bzura River fordable at this point.

Tum's *twelfth century basilica* is its principal monument. Though damaged in 1939 it has been rebuilt. The crypt is much older than the church. Baptismal fonts which have been found indicate that Christianity was practised here before A.D. 966 when it was first thought

133

to have been introduced into Poland. In the structure of the church traces of utensils and wild and domestic animal bones have been found.

The church, obviously built for defence as well as for worship, has three naves. In the walls at the lower levels are defensive loopholes, light being provided by windows set high up and difficult to reach. The towers too are set wide apart with loopholes at the base and centre.

During its early days the church was used for political and ecclesiastical conferences and was certainly one of the most impressive of the older churches seen on our travels.

The church treasury may also be visited. Close by you can also see a small wooden church typical of those found in parts of the Polish countryside.

INFORMATION FOR THOSE PLANNING TO STAY IN LODZ

(1) *How to Reach Lodz*

Take the through trains from Ostend or the Hook of Holland to Warsaw and then change to local rail services. Those travelling by air should fly to Warsaw and then continue the journey by rail. There are also local coach services operating between Warsaw and Lodz.

(2) *Hotels*

In 1st Class Category. Grand Hotel (334 beds) Avenue Piotrkowska 72. Phone 399-20. Hotel Polonia (216 beds) Avenue Narvtowicza 38. Phone 287-73. Hotel Savoy (254 beds) Avenue Travgutta 6. Phone 389-96.

In 2nd Class Category. Hotel Maly (34 beds) Avenue 22 Lipca 26. Phone 361-20.

In Tourist Category. Dom Wycieczkowy (74 beds) Avenue Przybyszewskiego 214. Phone 454-72.

(3) *Restaurants*

Halka. Avenue Moniuszki 1. (Dancing).
Tivoli. Avenue Tuwima 1. (Dancing).

(4) *Cafés*

Akademicka. Avenue Piotrkowska 108.
Lodzianka. Avenue Piotrkowska 74.
Cyganeria. Avenue Piotrkowska 29.

(5) *Shopping*

Lodz has some excellent shops, but these are the usual places for tourists to pick up purchases and they also accept Orbis coupons.
Ceplia. Avenue Piotrkowska 69. (Folk art).
Desa. Avenue Piotrkowska 117 and 133 (Antiques).
Jublier. Avenue Piotrkowska 74. (High class metal work).

(6) *Museums*

Historical Museum of the Textile Industry. Piotrkowska Avenue. (You will find this in an old factory next to the public gardens.)
Art Museum. Avenue Wieckowskiego 36.
Archaeological and Ethnographic Museum. Place Wolnosci (opposite the Town Hall).
Museum of the Working Class Struggle. Avenue Gdanska 3.

(7) *Theatres*

Lodz has several good ones including the 7.15; The Nowy; Mlodego Widza; Ziem Lodzkiej.

(8) *Cinemas*

Among the more centrally situated cinemas are the Adria and the Polonia on Avenue Piotrkowska and the Gdynia and Wisla on Avenue Tuwima.

(9) *Opera and Operetta*

Lodz has an opera house at Travgutta 18, while operettas are given at Avenue Piotrkowska 243.

(10) *Orbis*

There is an Orbis travel and exchange office at Avenue Piotrkowska 68. They can arrange local excursions, car hire and theatre and cinema tickets.

(11) *Post Office*

The main post and telegraph office at Avenue Tuwima 36/38 is open 24 hours a day.

PART V

CRACOW AND ITS SURROUNDINGS

CRACOW

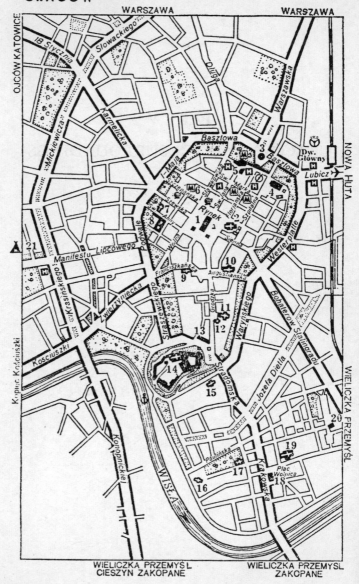

KEY TO CRACOW MAP

H = Hotels

M = Museums

1. Rynek Glowny (Market Square)
2. St. Mary's Church (Mariacki)
3. The Barbican and Florianska Gates
4. The Theatre
5. Czartoryski Museum
6. Szolayski House
7. St. Anne's Church
8. Collegium Maius
9. Franciscan Church
10. Dominican Church
11. Church of SS. Peter and Paul
12. St. Andrew's Church
13. Kanonicza Street
14. Wawel Castle and Cathedral
15. Bernardine Church
16. Church on the Rock
17. St. Catherine's Church
18. Ethnographic Museum
19. Corpus Christi Church
20. Old Synagogue
21. National Museum

CRACOW AND ITS SURROUNDINGS

CRACOW

As soon as you reach Poland someone will ask whether you have been to Cracow. The Poles who fervently cling to their cultural heritage are rightly proud of this lovely city which escaped wartime destruction to reflect everything that is glorious in Polish architecture. It is a city which should be included in every touring itinerary.

Like Warsaw, which in the sixteenth century supplanted Cracow as the Polish capital, it is sited on the River Vistula two hours by road or rail from the Carpathian mountains.

On the crossroads of main European trade routes, by the ninth century Cracow emerged as a leading European commercial centre, though it did not achieve capital status until the middle of the twelfth century.

The city is dominated by the Wawel Hill which was fortified to defend the crossing of the River Vistula which flows below. Its thirteenth century importance made it a target for the Tartars who continually raided it. In 1241 they captured and gutted the city, massacring most of the inhabitants. The city recovered quickly and was reconstructed with neatly angled streets surrounding an enormous city square.

Silesian settlers, Jews and Italians were brought in to repopulate it and by the middle of the fourteenth century it was more beautiful and prosperous than ever before.

This was Cracow's Golden Age. Kings were crowned and buried in the cathedral which had joined the castle on Wawel Hill. In 1364 Casmir the Great founded a university in the city which now became a renowned seat of learning. The wealth earned by trading was used by the merchants and bankers to build beautiful mansions and public monuments which are still standing. At the height of its Golden Age Cracow's population was around 300,000 people.

During the sixteenth century, after the discovery of America, with trade shifting from land to sea routes, Cracow's commercial importance began to be overshadowed. When, after a fire in Wawel Castle in 1595, Sigismund III decided to move the capital from Cracow to Warsaw the decline gained momentum to end in a series of epidemics and the destructive Swedish invasions of 1655–1657.

At the time of Poland's partition, Cracow was little more than a relatively unimportant Polish provincial city, though it did have a moment of greatness when in 1848 Tadeusz Kosciuszko from Cracow attempted an insurrection against the partitioning powers.

The Austrians, who as a partitioning power held Cracow, were not severe masters. Following a disastrous fire in the early twentieth century, Cracow once again started to expand into a prosperous community.

During the Second World War, Hans Frank, Nazi Gauleiter of Poland, lived like royalty in Wawel Castle which became the setting for wild abandoned parties. Although Cracow's treasures were looted and carried off to Germany, the city escaped the wanton excesses wreaked on other Polish towns, although only a surprise offensive by the Soviet army on January 18th 1945 saved the city from destruction by the retreating Germans who had already made plans to blow up the most important buildings including Wawel castle and cathedral.

Though there is much to see in Cracow, some of its finest treasures are not immediately obvious and have to be looked for, though it is best to begin your city sightseeing on Wawel Hill.

Seen from the river banks, *Wawel Hill* though dominated by the spires of its cathedral and castle does not seem particularly impressive or attractive, the red brick walls and green copper domes looking ordinary enough. In fact you are far more likely to be impressed by the concentration of the old men playing chess on the river bank opposite the castle.

Once you have climbed the slope and passed through the castle's red brick and creeper-covered gateway you reach a wide grass-covered forecourt surrounded on three sides by buildings.

To your left rises the bulk of the cathedral, with its cluster of cupola-ed side chapels, that of the Sigismund chapel with its gilded roof gleaming like beaten gold in the bright sunshine to catch your eye. Immediately ahead are some low undistinguished buildings built and used by the Austrians as barracks, but cutting off the view of the castle reached through the archway. Payment is made at the kiosk on the left as you enter.

Sticking through the forecourts' lawns are the foundations of a cruciform church demolished by the Austrians. Excavations are now taking place as it is thought that this could perhaps have been Poland's oldest church.

Wawel castle courtyard is among the world's most beautiful. Built in the early part of the sixteenth century, its two lower storeys are surrounded by lovely arcaded loggias, the top or third tier supported by tall slender colonnades designed to let the maximum amount of light into the top chambers during the grey Polish winters. Frescoes set high on the walls beneath the protruding roofs add splashes of gay colour to the cream painted walls. It is not difficult to imagine these beautiful loggias filled with people during the famous tournaments held here in the sixteenth century.

The courtyard like much of the present castle was the work of two Italian Renaissance architects, Francesco and Berecci. A tour through their beautifully designed and proportioned castle is something you will not readily forget.

To get the feel of the place begin by visiting the *Royal Treasury and Armoury* to be found in the remains of the old Gothic palace. Entrance is through the small door to the left of the staircase immediately ahead of you on entering the courtyard. In the treasury you will see gilt and silver plates and goblets, sceptres, miniatures, helmets, the winged armour of King John Sobieski III's hussars, shields, flintlocks with magnificent ornamentation, the rich gold robe given by Louis XIV of France to King John Sobieski III to commemorate his victory over the Turks at Vienna. In the light everything glints and gleams and is all quite beautiful.

Among all the treasures, the object most likely to be remembered is the coronation sword or 'Szczerbiec' not because it is of gold, but for its recent history. Looted during the Polish Partition, it was carried off to Germany and remained there for more than fifty years. After World War II it found its way to England to be offered for sale by public auction.

Poles living in England, afraid this historic piece would vanish into a private collection and for ever be lost to Poland, donated money so the sword might be bought by Poles who appreciated its sentimental and historic value to their country.

At first the emigré Poles who had bought the sword decided to keep it in one of their British communities—

but patriotism being a strong point even in exile, it was eventually agreed to send the sword back to Poland where it rightly belonged and it was added to the castle treasury.

Entering the main palace (in an ante-room you are given felt overshoes, but as there is plenty of highly polished marble on the floors and staircases take care), you are struck by the high airy rooms, the rich ornamentation of the portals, the huge earthenware stoves with their brilliantly coloured and beautifully glazed tiles and sixteenth century furniture.

The doors of inlaid walnut are also attractive, but these are post-war additions replacing the originals which were inlaid with mother of pearl and far more lovely, only time and Austrian and German garrisons had chipped and carved them so badly that they could not be saved.

The great feature of Wawel is the priceless collection of huge *sixteenth and seventeenth century tapestries* which decorate chamber after chamber filling them with riotous colour. The Poles claim these tapestries to be unequalled anywhere in the world, and I am quite prepared to believe them. They are magnificent.

One series is based on biblical themes, another larger series is devoted to animals, this series being commissioned by King Sigismund Augustus who was happiest on the hunting field and liked to have reminders of hunting around him.

The Poles being adept at showing their national treasures to the best advantage, most of the chambers have been hung with tapestries and refurnished in such a way that you can almost sense the presence of the kings and their courts who lived out splendid colourful lives in the series of apartments you are visiting.

Among the more interesting chambers are those on

the higher floors. These include the rooms of King Sigismund III who fancied himself as an alchemist. The walls are covered by luxurious inlaid Spanish leather and are almost barbaric in their splendour.

More impressive is the vast *Chamber of Deputies* with its huge biblical tapestries and the great coffered ceiling dating from 1535 with its thirty sculpted wooden heads of people belonging to the court of the time. There is nothing quite like this ceiling. All those little black frames with white plaster heads offered by the Polish souvenir shops are replicas of this unusual ceiling.

Do not leave Wawel without going to the very top floor to see the *Turkish Tents*. Captured at the great Battle of Vienna, the tents have been re-erected and cunningly floodlit so you can appreciate their beauty and colour.

The interior walls are covered with appliqué work in designs similar to those found on Persian carpets. In fact the floors of the tents were originally covered with Persian rugs and carpets, some of which were captured and can also be seen in these wonderful tents which glow in scarlets, golds, greens and turquoise.

Other top floor rooms offer collections of *Japanese* and *Ming pottery* for, after the Battle of Vienna, in Poland it was 'en vogue' to copy Oriental fashions, customs and habits. Among the nobility this fashion persisted for a considerable period, that is why so many seventeenth and eighteenth century portraits of the Polish nobility show them in faintly eastern dress.

We certainly loved Wawel castle and felt that to see it was worth our journey to Cracow. But we found *Wawel Cathedral* no less interesting.

The present fourteenth century Gothic building is the third cathedral to be built on Wawel Hill. All that remains of earlier cathedrals is an eleventh century crypt.

On entering, you are impressed by its proportions, but realise the symmetry has been spoiled by too many monuments, tombs and plaques put there in subsequent centuries. In fact in its way it is as cluttered with monumental bric-à-brac as our own Westminster Abbey.

In the right aisle is the tomb of Casimir Jagiello built between 1492–1496 and the work of Wit Stowsz. The recumbent figure is beautifully done.

Between the second and third pillars is the tomb of another Jagiello—Ladislaus—and dates from 1440, while the sandstone tomb of Casimir the Great built between 1370 and 1380—the third tomb in the right aisle—is equally impressive. Opposite in the left aisle is the tomb of Ladislaus the Short (1341–1346).

The great black crucifix which you will see, is the one from which the figure of Christ is said to have spoken to Queen Jadwiga telling her to marry Jagiello, the Lithuanian Grand Duke, so that by her marriage Lithuania would be converted to Christianity.

Of the many side chapels two are worth noting. The *Sigismund Chapel* is a real masterpiece considered one of the finest Renaissance monuments in Northern Europe with its tombs of red marble set against white marble walls.

The work of the Florentine Bartolomeo Berecci, it was begun in 1519 but took a team of thirty Italian and Polish workmen eleven years to complete.

The *Chapel of the Holy Cross* on the right immediately after entering the cathedral has some beautiful fifteenth century Ruthenian frescoes, quite colourful and unique in Poland.

Note too the elaborate *Tomb of St. Stanislaus*, patron saint of Poland. This is in the middle of the nave so cannot be overlooked.

In the eleventh century *vaulted crypt* which you can visit are the bodies of fourteen Polish kings, their wives and children, including King John Sobieski III and Stephen Batory, as well as the tombs of Poland's heroes.

Before leaving Wawel Hill take a look across the city and countryside. If you wish to buy cards or souvenirs there is a Ceplia shop in the forecourt by the entrance into the castle. There is also a public toilet close to the shop and signposted with a double O (OO).

Leaving Wawel Hill walk down *Kanonicza Street*, one of the city's oldest and most beautiful thoroughfares lined with the palaces and courtyards of rich merchants and noblemen. The view up Kanonicza Street, with Wawel's pinnacles towering above the houses with their richly ornamented doorways, is one of the most satisfying to be found in Cracow.

Kanonicza Street leads you into *Grodzka Street* by *St. Andrews Church*. Built in 1086 it was a fortress as well as a church and, powerful enough to withstand the Tartar onslaught of 1241, it escaped destruction.

Grodzka Street is now one of Cracow's main shopping streets, its pavements full of bargain hunters and tourists. But do not be deceived by outward appearances and pop up some of those narrow passages between the shops.

We did this although we at first thought they led into people's houses; we found they opened out into tiny courtyards with balconied houses and little shops and workshops. It was as though we had stepped back in time. What made our discovery more interesting was to find each courtyard had its own distinctive architecture and character.

Grodzka Street leads you into Cracow's huge market place, the *Rynek Glowny*, opposite the tiny twelfth century *Church of Sw. Wojcie* (St. Adelberts) built of great stone blocks surmounted by a small cupola.

The Rynek Glowny, one of Europe's largest town squares, has several outstanding monuments. The one which you immediately notice is the *Sukiennice* or *Cloth Hall* whose architecture is interesting.

The original having in 1555 been damaged by a great fire, two Italian architects Gian Maria Padovano and Santi Gucci were given the job of restoration. Because the Italians disliked steep sloping roofs, very necessary where heavy winter snows are to be expected, they overcame the difficulty by the creation of what has come to be known as the 'Polish Attic'—the steep slope of the roof being hidden behind a false front wall. Those of Cracow's Cloth Hall are particularly fine with great stone gargoyles looking down on to the flower sellers and the passing crowds.

The Cloth Hall is surrounded by arcades leading into small shops and to the popular *Sukiennice Coffee House* with its red plush, gilded woodwork and great mirrors. Those seeking public toilets will find one under the arcades at each end of the Cloth Hall.

Down the centre of the dimly lit and vaulted hall are rows of small booths where you can buy the usual tourist bric-à-brac, although the majority of articles offered for sale were of poor quality and inclined to be expensive. Still it was gay and colourful, almost like an eastern bazaar.

Midway, the hall is cut in half by a passage way. On the side nearest the Mickiewicz monument you will see an old blunt iron knife hanging from a chain.

According to local legend this knife is connected with the building of the nearby Church of St. Mary on which two brothers worked. The elder was a hard worker and his spire grew quickly. The younger, envious of his

148

brother's progress, took this knife and killed him. That far the tale seems pretty authentic—but the legend seems to have two very different endings.

One ending tells how the murdered man's tower began to shoot miraculously upwards and was capped with the lovely lace-like cupola seen today. The second version makes the fratricide's tower the taller and ends with the murderer making his confession from the tower top, stabbing himself with the same knife before jumping to his death.

No matter which is the true story, two things are certain, the knife on its chain and at St. Mary's Church two towers of differing height.

The Cloth Hall's first floor, now a branch of *Poland's National Museum*, is devoted to a large collection of Polish contemporary painting and well worth visiting.

The tall tower you can see behind the Cloth Hall is all that now remains of the *fourteenth century Town Hall* demolished in 1820 by the Austrians.

In a corner of the market place is the *Mariacki* or *St. Mary's Church*, built of red brick and with the irregular towers which are reputed to have caused the death of the two brothers.

But the taller spire has a yet more colourful legend with influences on Poland's present day life.

Every hour, especially at night when there is little noise, you can hear the soft silvery notes of a trumpet which seems to end its tune abruptly. This is the Heynal, a call which for several hundred years has been played every hour and always ends in this abrupt fashion.

Tradition has it that as Tartar raiders once entered the city while the people were at worship, a trumpeter stationed in the church tower saw them and immediately sounded the alarm on his silver trumpet. As the worshippers poured out of the church to defend themselves and their homes, the Tartars showered arrows at the church tower and one piercing the trumpeter's throat abruptly ended the alarm.

Saved by the warning, the citizens decided to remember the trumpeter by an hourly Heynal which would end abruptly on a strange high note. For Poland the Cracow Heynal is like the chimes of Big Ben. At noon when the Heynal is sounded it is radioed throughout Poland, the whole Polish nation setting their clocks and watches by it.

Entering the church which is built on a slightly lower level than the market place your eye is caught, even in the dim light, by the great *Triptych of Wit Stwosz*. This is not only the greatest single work of art in present day Poland, but an outstanding work of medieval artistry.

Made of beautifully carved wood, the central figures are life sized and show the Assumption of the Blessed Virgin Mary who is surrounded by the Apostles. The carving is so cunning and delicate that the figures seem almost life-like. The drapery of their robes is richly gilded and shines magnificently under the soft spotlights directed on to the Triptych to pick out the colours, especially the gilt. The wings of the Triptych, no less beautifully done, tell the story of Christ and the Virgin Mary.

In 1939 the Triptych was taken down and removed to Sandomierz so it should not be damaged. Discovered by the Germans it was carried off to Nuremberg and hidden in a mine. Found and returned to Poland, after restoration which required 64,000 working hours, it was re-hung in the Mariacki.

Above the Triptych are a series of gorgeous fourteenth century stained glass windows, and in the nave and choir nineteenth century frescoes which take up the themes and colours of the great Triptych.

In a side chapel is another great work of Wit Stowsz, a fine *crucifix*, the figure of Christ being so life-like it is obvious that this mediaeval artist knew a great deal about anatomy in an age when anatomic study was strictly forbidden.

Like all Polish churches the Mariacki, or Panna Marya as Cracow's citizens prefer to call it, is always full of silently praying Poles. Although ruled by the Communist system of government the people steadfastly cling to their Roman Catholic faith and it is not only the older generation who worship in the candlelit churches. We saw plenty of young students and children doing the same.

One of our more striking Polish memories is of a woman serving us in a Zakopane shop, who on hearing the noon church bell apologised and left us, while she went to kneel on the shop step facing in the direction of the church. After a few seconds of silent prayer she returned to complete her sale as though kneeling to pray on the doorstep was the most natural thing in the world.

From St. Mary's Church cross to the north side of the square and walk down *Florianska Street* with its small shops. Number 41 the house where Jan Matejko the Polish painter lived is now a museum, while Number 45 is the famous *literary café—Jana Michalikowa*—where young Polish intellectuals meet. Ahead you will see the *Florian Gate*, once the main city gate. Today with only a fragment of the city walls it still makes a brave show.

Immediately in front of it is a red brick *Barbican* which was also part of the fortifications. Small and semi-circular with seven slender turrets it is modelled on Arab military architecture and thought to have been designed by someone who returned to Cracow from the

Crusades. Once linked to the Florian Gate by a covered passageway and surrounded by a deep moat, they must together have been to an enemy almost impregnable.

Most of Cracow's fortifications were pulled down 150 years ago at the same time as the moat was filled to form the '*Planty*', a continuous strip of gardens encircling the old city to give it a touch of freshness as well as providing a lovely park for the citizens.

Walk westwards through the shady gardens or if you prefer it along the crowded and noisy boulevards Basztowa, 1 Maja and Podwale, before turning left into *St. Anny Street* which leads to the *Collegium Maius*—8/10 St. Anny Street—the oldest of Cracow's *University* buildings founded by Casimir the Great in 1364.

Do have a look at the Collegium which has a lovely courtyard surrounded by arcades and balconies somewhat after the style of Wawel but with fewer storeys not so grand.

You can get into the courtyard from Jagiellonska Street which also gives admittance to the *Jagiellonian Museum*, where among other things you can see an old globe showing the newly discovered American continent.

We were also shown a room named 'Alchemy'. In this room—or so we were told—Faust conducted his experiments and made his pact with the devil. In case we doubted the story we were shown a paw print on the stone floor and a clawed hand print burnt into the door.

We found you could spend a week in Cracow and not tire of its charms.

A large number of churches were visited by us. Those of the Franciscan Friars in Franciszanka Street and of St. Ann close to the Collegium Maius were well worth seeing, but it was Cracow's everyday life which interested us most.

Mornings were spent in the side-streets exploring

every nook and cranny, feeding the pigeons in the Rynek Glowny, mingling with the flower and fruit-sellers (in a countryside filled with orchards we were amazed by the poor quality of the badly speckled fruit offered for sale). Flowers also seemed expensive at our rate of exchange and I found myself paying 65 c. for a single red rose. In Cracow we also saw a considerable number of gipsies. The men seemed clean and nattily dressed, while their women folk favoured full, flower-printed chiffon skirts and deep fringed shawls. They earned their living as in other parts of the world by accosting passers-by for small change in return for wishes of good luck.

Though they were obviously a nuisance to most people we were glad to see the gipsies, a further proof of the failure of Hitler's extermination plan. We were perhaps more surprised to find beggars who stood outside the churches and on street corners. There were not all that many of them, but enough to be noticed which struck us as odd in a Communist society.

After the long late lunches favoured by the people of Cracow—2.00 p.m. did not seem an unusual time to begin eating the mid-day meal—we would stroll through the *Planty* gardens and end with a glass of tea and a plate of cakes at the Sukiennice Coffee House beneath the arcades of the Cloth Hall.

Though the service was painfully slow it gave us the chance to listen to the city's social chatter, observe the Polish old world etiquette of hand kissing and often to find ourselves drawn into conversation when it became known we were English.

Although in the late afternoon small queues formed outside in the hope of finding a free table in the Coffee House no one seemed to want to move and there was never any compulsion to get those who had been served

153

out to let others in. In fact most people seemed to spend at least two hours yarning.

After dark Cracow becomes another city. Though there is little neon, the shops are well lit and the main buildings softly spotlighted. Bookstalls seem to spring from the pavements and are quickly surrounded by armies of book browsers drawn from the large numbers of people promenading the streets. The soft-drink stands where cordial essence mixed with plain or soda water is popular at 50 groszys a glass usually have small crowds around them.

But the thing to do in Cracow after dark is to find one of the 'beat cellars' where Cracow's younger set gather to dance and flirt till the early hours. It is not unusual to find British beat groups performing. There was one in Cracow when we were there. Complete with Beatle hair-cuts, their appearance was a source of incredulous amusement though their music was appreciated and applauded.

Whereas many ancient cities do with time tend to become silent monuments, Cracow has no intention of letting this happen to her. We found the city as lively as they come, setting much of the pace followed by the rest of Poland.

No wonder the Poles are proud of Cracow, no wonder they stop to ask whether you have been there. In fact if you are in Poland you simply must go to Cracow. It is a city to which we will return.

INFORMATION FOR THOSE PLANNING TO STAY IN CRACOW

(1) *How to Get There*

Fast express trains link Cracow with Warsaw. You can also travel from Warsaw by coach or by domestic air services.

(2) *Hotels*

In S Category. Hotel Cracovia (677 beds) Avenue Poszkina 1. Phone 213-43. We stayed at the Cracovia finding it very comfortable but, being on the outskirts of the town which meant a fifteen minute walk, a tram or taxi to the town centre, not all that convenient.

Hotel Fracuski (90 beds) Avenue Pijarska 13. Phone 25-270.

In 1st Class Category. Grand Hotel (121 beds) Avenue Slawkowska 5. Phone 537-37. Hotel Polonia (150 beds) Avenue Basztowa 25. Phone 261-61. Hotel Pod Zlota Kotwica (114 beds) Avenue Szpitalna 30. Phone 560-00. Hotel Polski (90 beds) Avenue Pijarska 17. Phone 237-42. Hotel Dom Turysty (939 beds) Avenue Westerplatte 15. Phone 288-80.

In 2nd Class Category. Hotel Warszawski (75 beds) Avenue Pania 6. Phone 258-26. Hotel Europejski (113 beds) Avenue Lubicz 5. Phone 267-43.

In 3rd Class Category. Hotel Narodwy (59 beds) Avenue Poselska 22. Phone 509-00. Hotel Monopol (72 beds) Avenue Warynskiego 6. Phone 219-12. Hotel Pod Roza (141 beds) Avenue Florianska 14. Phone 576-14.

(3) *Restaurants*

If you like the opportunity to dance while you dine try:

Cyganeria—Avenue Szpitalna 38.

Kaprys—Avenue Florianska 32.

Francuski—Avenue Pijarska 13.

Grand—Avenue Slawkowska 5/7.

Restaurants without facilities for dancing include:

Wierzynek—Rynek Glowny 16.

Hawelka—Rynek Glowny 34.

Ermitage—Avenue Karmelicka 3.

Pod Zlota Kotwica—Avenue Szpitalna 30.
Warszawianka—Avenue 1 Maja 4.

(4) *Cafés*

Sukiennice—Rynek Glowny (In the Cloth Hall Arcades).
Feniks—Avenue Sw. Jana 2 (Dancing).
Jama Michalikowa—Avenue Florianska 45.
Literacka—Avenue Pijarska 7.

(5) *Students' Bars*

If you want a night out with Cracow's younger element try the Klub Pod Jaszczurami, Rynek Glowny 18.

(6) *Museums and Art Galleries*

Cracow's Museums are open daily except Monday and days following Public Holidays.

In addition to the Museums of Wawel and the National Museum in the Cloth Hall, the following are well worth devoting some time to.

Szolayskich Collection—Szczepanski Square 19. A museum devoted to Polish art of all periods including the famous Madonna of Kruzlowa.

Czartoryski Collection—Avenue Pijarska 15. Among the exhibits is Leonardo da Vinci's 'Lady with a Weasel' and the last work of Rembrandt 'Landscape with the Good Samaritan'.

Archaeological Museum—Jana Street 22.
National Science Museum—Avenue Slawkowska 17.
Pharmaceutical Museum—Basztowa Street 3.
Ethnographic Museum—Wolnica Square 1. Dealing with Polish Folklore and Folk Art.
Cracow Museum—Jana Street 12. This also includes some colourful folklore exhibits.

(7) Shopping

Cracow has plenty of good shops strung around the Rynek Glowny, along Grodzka Street, and in the main streets radiating from the Rynek Glowny.

Those wanting general souvenirs may find suitable pieces in the booths in the Cloth Hall or in the shops under the Cloth Hall arcades.

(8) Theatres

Dramatyczny—Place Sw. Ducha 1.
Sala Klubu ZZK—Avenue Sw. Filipa 6.
Stary—Avenue Jagiellonska 1.
Kameralny—Avenue Bohaterow Stalingradu 21.
Rapsodyczny—Avenue Skarbowa 2.
Rozmaitosci—Avenue Karmelicka 4.
Teatr '38'—Rynek Glowny 8.
Groteska—Avenue Sw. Jana 6.

(9) Cinemas

Uciecha—Avenue Bohaterow Stalingradu 16.
Wolnosc—Avenue 18 Stycznia 1.
Warszawa—Avenue Stradom 15.
Wanda—Avenue Warynskiego 7.
Apollo—Avenue Solskiego 2.

(10) Opera and Operetta

Muzyczny—Avenue Senacka 6.
Operetkowa—Avenue Lubicz 48.

(11) Zoo

The Cracow Zoo is to be found at Las Wolski.

(12) Post Office

The main post office is at Avenue Wielopole 2 and is

open from 8.00 a.m. to 8.00 p.m. You will find an all-night post office at the railway station.

(13) *Orbis*

The Orbis travel and currency exchange office is to be found at Szczepanski Square 3. Phone 2-40-33.

(14) *Long Distance Coaches*

You will find the coach station immediately in front of the railway station. Long distance coaches operate from Cracow to Warsaw, Poznan, Zakopane, Katowice, Sandomierz etc.

(15) *Motoring Information*

The Regional Office of the Polish Motoring Union is at Avenue Mikolajska 4. Phone 2-02-15.

The twenty-four hour petrol pump is sited at Avenue Pstrowskiego.

The Technical Repair Service (TOS) is at Avenue 29 Listopada 90. Phone 3-73-03.

NOWA HUTA

Five miles from Cracow, Nowa Huta or in English 'New Foundry' is a new industrial town which has grown up around the great Lenin Steelworks, the largest in Poland with an annual output of over two million tons.

The Poles are very proud of this new town which was founded in 1949 and today has 140,000 people. It is not a beautiful place, but what industrial towns are? You are bound to be interested in the great apartment blocks with gay-coloured balconies—orange is the predominating colour—the markets, big self-service stores and general air of prosperity even though you are left with the impression that the town is half finished and does not seem to have any centre.

Bus A from the Rynek Glowny will in fifteen minutes take you from old world Cracow to modern Nowa Huta.

We found plenty to interest us just wandering around the clinically clean streets, comparing the shops and living quarters with those of western Europe. We would like to have been able to compare prices but the odd tourist exchange rate made this impossible. However the shoppers did not seem to be short of money and our hour in Nowa Huta passed quickly enough.

WIELICZKA

Seven miles south-east of Cracow and reached by tram in little more than twenty minutes are the amazing salt mines of Wieliczka.

There is little to see on the journey except a good view across the River Vistula of Wawel and a new children's sanatorium built to a circular design set on a low hill looking across country to the distant chimneys of Nowa Huta. Money for this vast building was subscribed by Polish-Americans.

At Wieliczka there is little above ground to tell you there is a mine, just a low red brick building behind a green lawn surrounded by begonia beds with a miner's statue in the middle.

Records show that at Wieliczka salt has been mined commercially since the tenth century, though it is fairly certain it was being dug much earlier. During the Middle Ages the Wieliczka salt was very important to the Polish economy.

Daily from 10.00 a.m. to 5.00 p.m. there are conducted tours, the guides in their blue smocks with white helmets sitting on a seat at the entrance to the mine building waiting for sufficient visitors to assemble to form a party.

The guides were a friendly bunch. One had served in 301 Air Squadron during the Battle of Britain and was obviously delighted to receive British visitors—even a British teenager whose Beatle haircut caused a major sensation and bets as to what sex he might be.

You enter the mine by climbing down flights of steps to a depth of 180 feet. There is a lift, but that is only used to take you back to the surface.

Your visit begins in the *Mine Museum* 300 feet below the earth's surface which alone makes it unusual. Its exhibits range from clear salt crystals to date palm fronds and nuts embedded in crystal salt and explanations of how mining was done here in the Middle Ages.

Those who are uncomfortable below ground may find it nerve-racking walking along the mine tunnels, the roof supported by timber, but when the tunnels open into vast chambers with walls, ceilings, floors, altars, chandeliers all made of glittering salt crystals uneasiness quickly vanishes to be replaced by amazement.

Several chambers have been converted into chapels which were built over several centuries. *St. Anthony's Chapel* was carved in 1675, the *Holy Cross Chapel* also in the seventeenth century and the *St. Cunigonde Chapel* in the nineteenth century. The chambers are still being sculpted, Snow White and the Seven Dwarfs being one of the latest sets of figures to be completed.

One chamber known as the *Crystal Cave* is over 200 feet high and in the electric light sparkles with salt crystals. There are also mysterious salt lakes. In one, during the war, nine German soldiers drowned, having somehow strayed into it from the aircraft spare parts factory which the Germans opened up in the depths of

17. A peasant in the Podhale region, near Zakopane, blowing on a horn

18. A view over Zakopane to the Tatras

19. Winter at Zakopane—sunbathing on Gubalowka Mountain

20. Zakopane—cable car to Kasprow Wierch summit in winter

the mine. One chamber has been turned into a tennis court for the miners to use during rest periods.

There are nearly three miles of tunnels at Wieliczka. Being somewhat disabled I was soon in difficulties—but the guide realising the trouble lifted me on to his back and carried me up and down stairs and through the labyrinth so I should miss nothing. When I protested that I was too heavy, he shrugged it off with the remark that as we had travelled so far to get to Poland, it was little enough for him to do in return. No wonder we grew to like the Poles.

AUSCHWITZ (OSWIECIM)

Oswiecim, better known by its German name, Auschwitz, is 40 miles by road from Cracow.

It is a pleasant road winding through hills and woods, past villages of small thatched and timbered cottages whose beams are often picked out in eggshell blue paint.

The approach to Oswiecim is undistinguished, the road running beside a concrete fence half hiding a factory and marshalling yards. Tensed for our first glimpse of the Auschwitz Concentration Camp, we imagined this was it. But we had yet to go through the town where taking place at that moment was the funeral of a local dignitary.

Bells tolled in the tower of the fourteenth century church as the funeral procession headed by two boys carrying black flags went ahead of the cortège. They were followed by lads with scarlet cushions on which the medals of the dead man were to be seen. The choir wearing tiny black capes over their surplices were followed by a retinue of priests and pall bearers. The coffin carried high above the heads of the mourners was

F
161

covered in a rich black velvet pall embroidered with an elaborate pattern in silver thread.

As the procession passed our car, we watched the townsfolk fall in behind the mourners to form a long crocodile to the graveside of an obviously much loved man.

Behind the procession went the hearse, an ordinary black painted van, with funeral emblems picked out in gold paint. To us it seemed odd that our visit to Auschwitz where people were slaughtered in their millions, and where a factory for the processing of human bodies had been planned, should have begun in such a manner.

Do not for one moment imagine your first sight of the Auschwitz camp will shock you. It is possible to drive by without realising what it is. The road sign simply says 'museum'.

The camp is protected by a wire fence behind flower beds with a collection of comfortable looking tenements, fruit and tobacco kiosks, cafés and ice-cream stands close by.

The camp—or museum as the Poles prefer to call it—opens at 08.00 a.m., the last guided tour of the day with an English-speaking lecturer leaving the main gate at 2.00 p.m. You buy your entrance tickets at the main gate. Those with weak stomachs might at this stage be advised to use the toilets to the left of the ticket kiosk.

Your visit will be to the first and smallest of the three camps in the area, which collectively came to be known as Auschwitz. It opened in June 1940 and was originally an army barracks.

As the Nazis over-ran more and more of Europe this camp became far too small to handle all those sent there, so a second much larger camp—Brezinka or Birkenau—was specially designed and built on the other side of the railway line. Capable of holding 200,000 prisoners, this was a large wood and brick camp where men and women were segregated—there being two male prisoners to every female.

At Brezinka were the three large gas chambers and crematoria—one being hidden in the nearby woods.

The third camp—Dwory—was a labour camp, the inmates working in the chemical plant opened here by the I.G. Farben Industrie and kept running by a constant supply of young healthy prisoners. Those who showed signs of fatigue through malnutrition were soon disposed of in the gas chambers and crematoria.

As you move towards the red brick camp, to your left you will see a low black tarred building. This is the small gas chamber and crematorium, which was the pilot scheme for the larger ones which were to be built at Birkenau.

You get into the concentration camp itself through a wide gate surmounted by the words '*Arbeit Macht Frei*' —or 'Work for your Freedom'. Few who passed those gates were ever to be free again.

As you walk through the gates you cross a narrow no-man's-land between two barbed wire fences which once carried killer voltages of electricity. You can also see the guard towers with their searchlights as well as a large bird table where the guards placed titbits for the sparrows while human beings starved in front of them.

The conducted tour begins with a film in English. Shown in one of the three-storeyed red brick prison blocks, it shows the liberation of Auschwitz on January 27th 1945 when the Soviet army discovered 220,000 starving prisoners, all that was left of $4\frac{1}{2}$ million people from 29 countries who in four years had been carted by railway across Europe in cattle trucks to death in Auschwitz.

Having set the scene, the guide will take you through

the prison blocks, each of which tells a further part of the terrible Auschwitz story, the telling of which forms the museum.

There are the prison records with times and dates of executions. The gas containers—no more than tins with the marks of the tin openers still to be seen, as well as the small gas pellets which look like tiny pieces of grey flint. There is a child's broken doll—then more spectacular exhibits.

Down the entire wall of one large room behind a glass screen is a great mound of human hair. Cut from the heads of the dead, it used to be baled and sent to Germany to stuff cushions and mattresses.

Another window shows children's hair, still neatly plaited and tied with gay ribbons. Unless you happened to be a twin and so required for medical experiments, as a child you were of no use at Auschwitz and instantly destroyed.

A further window reveals scores of calipers, crutches and artificial limbs worn by the disabled to whom no mercy at all was shown. Like the small children they were immediately expendable.

There are mountains of steel spectacle frames, and the neatly labelled suitcases carried by the victims to Auschwitz. The children's tiny cases seem particularly touching.

There are mounds of clothing including that worn by children and babies as well as dummies on teething rings, mountains of shoes, hair, shaving and tooth brushes, while battered utensils seemed to fill an entire ground floor room overspilling into the cellars.

Standing looking at these everyday possessions of men, women, children and babies slaughtered without mercy, you will feel horror and anger sweeping over you.

But if these exhibits are not enough to move you,

there is also a collection of enlarged photographs, many taken by soldiers doing duty at the camp, to send home to their friends and families.

If the delivery to the camp had been a large one and the gas chambers were not immediately able to cope with the volume, to speed them to their death victims for the gas chambers were compelled to strip in the woods. In the photographs you can see them as they made their way naked through the trees towards the crematoria.

There are pictures of the arrival of the trains, the Nazi doctor with a gesture of his finger deciding by intuition who should go to the right for temporary survival in the Dwory or Birkenau camps. Those going left walked straight into the stripping rooms which meant death in less than an hour of arrival at Auschwitz.

The men seen in the photograph are mostly grey-headed with walking sticks. One does not need to guess their end, and yet one dodderer being led away is supported in a most touching fashion on the arm of a Nazi soldier.

The photo of the ashes of the crematoria with a man's head unburned, the features still distinct, is one which will always haunt my memory and caused a great deal of distress among members of our guided party.

So did Block Number 10 which showed some of the inhuman experiments on women, while Block Number 11, which apart from having been cleaned up, is as it was during the war.

Here you can see the Block Commandant's room with his steel helmet and truncheon on the desk, his bed in a corner. Opposite is a committee room where prisoners for death were selected.

Here too is the place where the prisoner trusties lived in comparative comfort while next door are the dormitories with the three-tiered bunks hopelessly crowded together. In a room approximately 20 feet square we estimated something like seventy prisoners at a time lived, ate, slept and died. Opposite was a small washing trough and a single pedestal type toilet.

We went into the cellars to see the special cells for rebellious prisoners awaiting execution. One tiny room had space for four men provided they spent their days and nights standing bolt upright. In another you will see the cell in which forty men at a time shared a single toilet, found light and air from a grille no more than six inches square. In winter when it was snow-blocked, the men in danger of suffocation had with their finger-nails picked a small breathing hole in the cell door which the guide will point out to you.

Prisoners living in this particular cell were rarely fed. Condemned to death, to their guards it hardly seemed to matter if the prisoners died of starvation, gas or the executioner's bullet. At least one recorded case of cannibalism took place in this room.

The small ground floor cell with the untidy heap of clothes on the floor and the rusty urinal trough in the corner is where prisoners stripped naked before being taken for execution in the yard of Block 11. Robbed of the last shreds of human dignity which a scrap of cloth to cover their nakedness might have given them, the condemned knelt to face a black metal plate fixed to the brick wall while the revolver which was to blow their head asunder was pressed against the cranium.

You will see the wall and the metal plate, but today its base is piled, high with wreaths and flowers. The Poles remember those who died at Auschwitz and keep faith with posies of flowers, replacing them as soon as they begin to fade.

The memorial to the four million dead is near the

gate. It is quite simple—a small block of black marble inscribed 1940–1945.

From the small camp we drove to the remains of Birkenau. You will find a forest of brick chimneys is all that remains of the wooden shacks in which the prisoners lived and which were burned down after the liberation.

You can inspect, as we did, the gas chambers and crematoria blown up by the retreating Nazis. You may also wish to stand on the platform where the prisoners left those ghastly cattle trucks at the end of those terrible rail journeys.

Standing there with the light rapidly fading as the swift Polish evening began to fall, we looked, as so many prisoners must have looked, at the tall poplars swaying in the early autumn breeze, finding it hard to believe that such a concentration of horror had happened at this spot.

You will find it impossible to prevent yourself from asking a hundred and one unanswerable questions. How had all this happened? Why choose an insignificant little town like Oswiecim for this ghastly experiment with death? What kind of men could spend days at their drawing boards perfecting plans for a rapid execution chamber capable of gassing and burning people in their tens of thousands, for here everything was planned with meticulous detail. It did not happen by accident.

And what were the emotions of those men and women who manufactured and packed the gas pellets, or sorted those bales of human hair when it reached Germany? Did they ever stop to ask questions?

These were the type of questions which piled up as on our drive back to Cracow we talked about Auschwitz.

Auschwitz is not a nice place to visit. Understandably children are not allowed in. Many women in our party

167

were unable to stomach everything they saw and retired from the party.

Yet everyone agreed that Auschwitz museum should be seen by every person visiting South Poland for Auschwitz must never be forgotten just in case forgetfulness allows it all to happen again.

PART VI
POLAND'S MOUNTAINS

POLAND'S MOUNTAINS

Along her southern border with Czechoslovakia and
the Soviet Union Poland has her mountains which
though not as spectacular as the Alps are pleasant
enough.

THE BIESZCZADY MOUNTAINS

In the south-east are the Bieszczadys with peaks rising
to around 3,000 feet. Part of the Carpathians, they are
popular with those Poles wanting to get away from the
main tourist track.

Few foreign tourists have penetrated into this lonely
area of boulder-strewn heights, wooded glades and
turbulent streams running downhill through deep
forests towards the San river.

One of Poland's more primitive areas, there are few
villages but those that you do see as the overgrown
footpaths and country roads open into the hamlets are
always interesting, the little wooden houses clustered
around small wooden Orthodox churches with onion-
shaped steeples and simple shrines with nosegays of
fresh forest flowers.

The whole Bieszczady area is a nature park with
plenty of wild animals including bears, wolves and wild
cats. Its rivers teem with fish. Care has to be taken when
sunbathing as there are many poisonous snakes which
like the sun as much as you do.

Most Poles camp out in this area which has little
tourist accommodation. Though there are marked paths,
unless you are an experienced walker it would be better

to stay in one area and take some easy strolls rather than go on foot too far into an area where even the marked paths get overgrown and human habitations are few. It is also necessary to carry food supplies as shops are scattered.

Hostels are to be found in Baligrod, Ustrzyki Gorne and Komancza. Sanok has a small hotel—the Miejski—at Swierczewskiego 14.

Even those travelling by car may find the going difficult after they leave Lesko or Baligrod, though the road does in fact go as far as Ustrzyki Gorne where the main tourist paths start.

A beautiful area, yes, but strictly for nature lovers prepared to camp out and rough it while getting well and truly off the beaten track.

THE PIENINY MOUNTAINS

The Pieniny mountains rise from the rolling green foothills which sweep south from Cracow towards the higher peaks of the Tatras. They are quite compact, and most tourists visiting Zakopane end by seeing something of them while travelling by raft down the tortuous Dunajec river.

We travelled by road from Zakopane to Czorsztyn, a distance of some thirty miles through pastoral scenery with the typical wooden villages of this area which is known as the Podhale. The wooden chalets with their steep roofs are beautifully proportioned with the roofs made of small wooden pantiles which shine in the sun like silver fish scales. The men of the Podhale are great craftsmen with wood.

All over the area between the Pieniny and Tatras mountains the countrymen continue to wear their strange but colourful local costume with flat black-brimmed hats, the band made of white cowrie shells sewn on to red leather. Their white felt trousers embroidered on the thighs and crutch with bright coloured wools are supported by wide leather belts decorated with metal discs. White shirts with balloon sleeves are caught at the wrist by embroidered cuffs. On their feet they wear moccasins made from a single piece of leather often held to the feet by thongs around the ankles.

The woollen trouser embroidery differs between villages and it is possible for local people by glancing at it to know from which village or area the man comes.

On Sundays embroidered sheepskin jackets are worn, or white felt jackets embroidered in wool and worn over the shoulders like capes.

As popular with young men as with their elders, this unusual and colourful costume is likely to survive.

Before reaching Czorsztyn we took a right-hand track into the little somewhat scattered village of Debno to look at its wooden church.

DEBNO

Built in the fifteenth century, Debno church is made entirely from larch wood.

From the track we walked down a rough path, crossed the wooden bridge over a small stream and passed through the covered lych gate into the church-yard.

Clear of the surrounding trees we were able to see the church which has deep overhanging eaves, sloping walls, a square tower and a roof covered with wooden shingles.

The inside is most unusual being panelled in wood which has been carved into lace-like tracery and coloured in reds and blues. The ceiling is also painted with birds and Tudor style roses making up part of the design.

There are many small carved objects worth noting, especially the statue of the Madonna and the crucifix above a small side altar on your right.

The unusual wooden tracery and the primitive use of colour made Debno a church we were glad to have seen.

A great deal of work went into the building of the church, work so obviously done by skilled and dedicated hands, it was surprising to be told that they were the hands of a band of robbers who in the fifteenth century plundered and terrorised the district.

THE DUNAJEC

A voyage down the Dunajec is a highlight of a visit to South Poland. It is a picturesque and unusual voyage and we found it far more interesting than trips we have made on far more famous rivers.

On reaching Czorsztyn make for the landing stage opposite the Niedzica castle which crests the rocky tree-covered cliff. If you have time you can cross the river bridge and climb to the castle.

Built in the fourteenth century and carefully restored it was one of Poland's strongest frontier fortresses and according to a well authenticated story Princess Umina a member of Peru's last Inca royal family died in the castle and was buried in the chapel. How she got from Peru to this out of the way spot, no one seems to know.

At the Dunajec landing stage you will join other tourists waiting for the river trip, the journey being carried out by flotillas of rafts one following the other at short intervals.

Though described as rafts the craft are made of four hollowed poplar trunks held together at the front and back by strong saplings, foliage packed between the trunks making the rafts reasonably watertight. The seats are loose wooden planks across the top of the logs, your feet resting in the hollows; not altogether comfortable for a three-hour river journey, but such is the interest of the river you hardly notice the hard seats.

The rafts hold twelve people seated in three rows of four, and are poled down the river by two boatmen in local Podhale dress, one steering at the front the other from the rear.

As the flotilla sets out on the journey a village band plays them away from the landing while mid-stream, on two platforms, photographers snap the rafts as they sail by. A few hundred yards further on a gipsy stands in water up to his thighs playing a violin in the hope of earning a few coins.

On the Dunajec trip you get plenty of thrills without any real danger. A mainly shallow river, sometimes the raft scrapes the river bottom as the boatmen pole it through the small rapids, the water foaming and swirling against the rocks.

Those seated on the outside should wear light mackintoshes as, at times, the water splashes on to the raft and you can get wet.

For the first few miles the river flows through open, gently undulating pastoral country with Czechoslovakia to the right and Poland to the left, the river forming the boundary. Small riverside villages and the rapids keep what might be considered a dull stretch interesting, the most magnificent part of the trip being from Sromowce Nizne to Szczawnica.

Leaving Sromowce Nizne with a model of a stork set in a tree beside the river as a joke for travellers, the rafts pass below the massive and impressive Trzy Korony (Three Crowns) a 3,000 foot mountain and, turning

175

suddenly, enter what is known as the Pieniny Gate between the Grabczycha (left-hand side) and the Gora Klasztorna peaks.

The scenery now becomes outstanding, the dark green river flowing below high cliffs and crags often covered in rich forest. Sometimes the river is almost motionless, then in an instant and for a few hundred yards it boils and foams. Only the expert skill of the two boatmen saves the raft from being dashed to pieces on submerged rocks or against the cliff walls.

In this stretch the boatmen will point out a spot called Zbojnicki Skok or 'robbers' leap' where recruits seeking a life of profitable crime were forced to leap across the river to test their courage and fitness.

This is also the part of the river where the boatmen point to distant rocks asking passengers whether they are on the Czech or Polish side of the river. Most passengers guess wrongly as the Dunajec is so serpentine that unless you are familiar with each short stretch it is impossible to tell which way it will go next.

Three hours may seem a long time to be on a raft. Before doing the trip we thought so too—but we would assure you that it passed surprisingly quickly with hardly a dull moment.

True, it was a nice day with bright sunshine. On a dull day with any hint of rain it would be best to forget it as the rafts are without cover and if it did rain it would be impossible for them to find shelter.

On landing at Szczawnica the photos taken from the mid-river platforms as we left Czorsztyn were offered for sale at 10 zlotys each.

The cost of the river trip was 50 zlotys, hardly a cheap trip but worth every penny, as to get the rafts back to the starting point at the end of their long journey the boatmen have to begin taking the rafts to pieces, loading the hollow trunks on to horse-drawn carts before driving back to Czorsztyn.

It turned out to be a trip which we would very much like to do again.

THE PIENINY TRAIL

Those who like walking can as an alternative to the Dunajec trip tackle the Pieniny trail from Czorsztyn to Szczawnica. Although it is only about twelve miles, as it crosses the summits of several mountains the going is not always easy and you need to allow at least nine hours which gives ample time for rests and to admire the wonderful views of the Dunajec from the mountains.

Where the road branches at Czorsztyn take the blue marked track past Czorsztyn castle which gives the first river views. Continue along the path through the village of Nadzamcze and walk the crest of the mountains through a pleasing countryside of woods and meadows with some rocky outcrops.

Bypass the village of Haluszowa and still following the marked path go forward to the Szopka pass where you will get a fine view of the distant Tatras mountains. Now follow the road to the Trzy Korony (Three Crowns) mountain. At its summit is a gallery reached by climbing some wooden steps. The view is magnificent, embracing the Dunajec gorge as well as the Tatras.

Go downhill to Korsarzysko and continue past the castle to Zamkowa Gora where you again enjoy a view. The path crosses the meadows and passes through the woods over the Potok Pieninski stream before climbing to the mountain crest. By continuing along the crest you get good views of the mountains and the Dunajec. From the top of Czertezik (2,316 feet) follow the path through the forest and to the summit of Sokolica for yet another fine view of the Dunajec.

From Sokolica walk down the right-hand path at the road fork which takes you to the river. After a short walk along its bank you reach Szczawnica.

This walk takes you through the finest parts of the Pieniny mountains and is in fact the route through the Pieniny National Park. Remember to take plenty of food as there is no chance of buying any en route. Stout walking shoes or boots are an essential too.

Anyone wishing to stay in the Pieniny area will find accommodation at the Hotel Schroncsko Orlica in Szczawnica.

THE TATRAS MOUNTAINS

Driving south from Cracow to Zakopane as you ascend the hills before dropping down to Nowy Targ you can in the distance see the rugged peaks of the Tatras.

The Tatras split themselves into two parts. These ridges forming the High Tatras are of granite, the Western Tatras being limestone.

There are few gentle slopes in these mountains which seem to fall almost vertically to the valley floor, the higher rock walls devoid of greenery. Towards their base they are covered with very thick pine forests. Motoring through the Tatras with the granite rock walls thrusting above the trees we were reminded of pictures of the Canadian Rockies, though unlike Canada unless you go in the early spring you will find no snowy peaks, the only snow being the remains of winter avalanches caught in sheltered gulleys. There are also no glaciers in the Tatras to provide a touch of alpine majesty.

Even so they are impressive mountains and climbers find it very tough going when tackling their rock walls and serrated ridges.

ZAKOPANE

Zakopane is the most popular Tatras holiday spot and one of Poland's leading international tourist centres.

Our first impression of Zakopane was not altogether favourable. Perhaps we were looking for something cosmopolitan and scenically striking. Zakopane is neither.

It lies in an open green valley, the protecting Gubalowska ridge lying to the north and the 6,000 foot high Giewant to the south. Maybe our initial disappointment was due to the fact that the mountains have receded, but as the days passed we realised Zakopane had character and was as pleasant a resort as you will find in any mountains.

To begin with it is not a small place. Its population is somewhere around 23,000, but the town being scattered over the valley floor you never get the impression of its size until you take the mountain railway up to Gubalowska.

Most of the town is stretched along Krupowki and its Zamoyskiego extension lined with small souvenir shops selling wooden boxes, plates and such like. All through the day these streets are jam packed with tourists wandering up and down peering into shop-windows or going into cafés and restaurants for coffee or ice-cream.

Promenading with the crowds you begin to realise Zakopane should not be dismissed by too hasty a judgement. Among the people you will see costumed highlanders, their gaily embroidered white felt trousers lending splashes of colour. Then there are their wives whose great baskets are caught up in white sheets knotted over their shoulders for easy carrying.

Follow them as they move north along Krupowki Street in the direction of Gubalowska and you will find that where Krupowki and Koscielisko Streets join there are two small *open air markets*.

That to your left across the wooden bridge over the stream is for fruit, flowers and farm produce. It is a 'free market' where countrywomen in their pleated and flowered skirts, deep fringed shawls worn over their head and mouths, sell cheese made from ewe's milk, bilberries, wild strawberries and eggs.

The appearance of the cheeses is interesting. Made by pouring sour cream into wooden moulds decorated with geometric designs, when the moulds are opened the hardened cheese is waxed and with the impression of the exotic design from the mould stamped on to them they looked quite unlike any cheese we had seen.

Some of the larger cheeses weighed several pounds and cost about 40 zlotys, but there were also complete cheeses in size hardly bigger than an egg. They too were embossed with strange designs and cost around 2 zlotys.

Zakopane's second market is equally interesting. Countrywomen are again the chief merchants selling the mohair wool cardigans which they have knitted. As they stand, their merchandise piled in front of them, they knit or else with a brush bring up the nap on the articles they are selling. Here there is also a flourishing market in second-hand garments and for the primitive but distinctive leather moccasins worn by the highland people.

When you are at the market spare a few minutes to look at the *old wooden church* and the *highlanders' houses* which are close by in Koscielisko Street.

At Number 10 Krupowki Street, almost opposite the new stone church and lying back from the road is the *Tatras Museum* which is worth a visit.

Inside are a series of local costumes, a reconstruction of a highlander's cottage interior—note the cradle suspended over the bed so the parents can swing the baby to sleep without having to get out of bed in the bitter Polish winters—specimens of all the mountain plants and flowers as well as cases filled with stuffed birds and animals which are native to the Tatras.

The museum is small but extremely interesting and an hour spent there goes quickly.

As in all popular mountain resorts, Zakopane has its man dressed in a polar bear skin to encourage tourists to have their photograph taken with him.

Once we had managed to find our way around the scattered town we discovered Zakopane was not short on entertainment with dancing, cinemas, concert halls and sports stadia.

The main reason for the popularity of Zakopane is that it is such a good centre to get around from.

A pleasant way to spend an afternoon is to take the funicular from the north end of Krupowki Street to the top of *Gubalowka*. The ascent takes about fifteen minutes, but when you get to the top and step on to the green terraces with plenty of wooden seats where you can sit to admire the Tatras ranges with Zakopane spreading below, you realise what a wonderful vantage point it is. There is a restaurant and bar.

If you do not want to go back by train to Zakopane you can walk down by following the black marked path by the railway, through the village of Gladkie until it brings you out by the old wooden church in Koscieliska Street.

The trip to the top of *Kasprowy Wierch* (6,522 feet) is more exciting. You can begin by either walking the $2\frac{1}{2}$ miles from the town centre to Kuznice or by taking a bus. It is an easy walk past smart villas and the new Hotel Zakopane, after which the road enters the forest until it ends at the cable-car station at Kuznice.

The journey in the aerial gondola skimming the forest tree tops is spectacular. After changing gondola cars at the half-way station the final section with the gondola seeming almost to touch the rugged granite chimneys is thrilling.

The whole journey takes little more than twenty minutes, the cable car ascending at sixteen feet a second to a height of 6,426 feet. At the summit there is a restaurant and souvenir shop. The restaurant has a sun terrace overlooking a splendid view of rugged barren peaks which surround you on all sides. There are several good footpaths leading from the restaurant to the mountain ridges and by following them you quickly cross into Czech territory.

Dolina Koscieliska a picturesque valley five miles from Zakopane is another popular short excursion. You can get a bus to the start of this three-mile-long valley which is one of the most spectacular in the Tatras with its rocky chimneys, torrents, forests and ravines. Provided you have some stout walking shoes and a picnic lunch you can spend a glorious day among the beautiful scenery which encloses this valley.

If you want to cut down on the walking, there are horse-drawn fiacres from the bus stop up to *Polarna Pisna* but you will then have to walk to the Hala Ornak Hostel.

Another popular walk is in the *Bysta Valley*. After going on foot or by bus to Kuznice you take the steep path to *Kalatowki* where you will find a hostel with a bar and restaurant. It takes just over an hour to get there.

But perhaps the most outstanding of the many mountain excursions is that to *Morskie Oko*.

Buses leave from Zakopane taking the excellent road southwards into the Tatras National Park. Passing through the small village of Jaszczurowka as the road climbs and turns just before entering the forest on your left you will see a very elaborately designed wooden church, though it is of no great age.

The ride through the thick forest is wonderful. You can see foresters at work cutting and hauling timber, and you may, like us, be lucky enough to see a few deer crossing the road. But it will be the density of the tree trunks which will impress you most. They grow so very close together that in places they have cut out the light.

Beyond *Cyrhla Toporowa* from where you get a good view of the Zakopane valley, the road twists and climbs before dropping down to *Lysa Polona* where the shallow river flows down the forested valley to form the frontier between Poland and Czechoslovakia. Here there is an attractive and impressive customs post with a petrol station close by. It is reasonably busy, many Czech touring coaches crossing here to tour the Tatras National Park and to visit Morskie Oko.

The road now enters upon its most beautiful stretches with thick forest on either side and ahead the granite peaks of the rocky amphitheatre in which Morskie Oko lies.

At *Wodogrzmoty Mickiewicza* it passes above a torrent with the water plunging over a series of rocky ledges to the valley floor. Shortly afterwards unless you have a special permit you have to leave your wheeled transport to walk about a mile to Morskie Oko.

Morskie Oko is the largest lake in the Tatras surrounded by no less than fifteen peaks of more than 6,800 feet including Rysy, the highest peak of the Tatras.

The name Morskie Oko means 'the eye of the sea', local legend maintaining that the lake is connected to the sea by a series of subterranean passages.

The barren granite mountain walls encircling the lake are very impressive especially when reflected in its own grey waters which are so clear that you can see the lake bed.

To reach the lakeside you have to walk down a series of rough stone steps. At the foot there is usually a cluster of countrywomen selling wooden souvenirs, wild strawberries or other fruits.

You are bound to follow other visitors to the edge of the small boat jetty to throw a coin into the lake presumably for luck. The lake bed is thick with coins not only at this spot but at several points round the lake which tourists have taken a fancy to.

For 2 zlotys you can be rowed across the lake—it is not very big by other standards—to climb up a rocky track where you can look down on a second smaller lake. Known as Czarny Staw or the Black Lake it is hidden behind a ridge. You can reach this second lake by following a well marked path along the eastern shore of Morskie Oko.

At Morskie Oko there is a PTTK Hostel with 40 beds. It also provides meals for day-trippers as well as coffee and soft drinks. Though its accommodation is very much on the simple side it does offer a spectacular view of the lake and the surrounding mountains.

We thought Morskie Oko wild, impressive and beautiful. It would be a pity if you missed it.

Zakopane is of course Poland's outstanding Winter Sports resort. It has three good ski jumps, special championship and slalom slopes, ski li fts, cable cars, a ski school and facilities for ice skating.

INFORMATION FOR THOSE PLANNING TO STAY IN ZAKOPANE

(1) *How to Get There*

By through train from Ostend **or the Hook** of

Holland to Warsaw. From Warsaw you can take through trains to Zakopane, though many travellers prefer to take the train only as far as Cracow, taking a coach from the bus terminus opposite the railway station to Zakopane. The distance by road is 66 miles and it is a pleasant scenic journey.

Air travellers can use the domestic flights from Warsaw to Cracow continuing from Cracow by rail or road.

(2) *Hotels*

In S Category. Hotel Giewont (76 beds) Avenue Kosciuszki 1. Phone 20-11. This is an old-established mountain hotel which we considered to be very comfortable.

In 1st Class Category. The Hotel Zakopane. A new hotel opened in the summer of 1965, it is sited on the southern edge of the town looking towards the mountains.

Dom Turysty (637 beds). Avenue M. Zaruskiego 5. Phone 32-81. A tourist grade PTTK hotel in a very quiet position a few yards from the town centre.

Hotel Swit (42 beds) Avenue Zamojskiego 20. Phone 16-34.

Hotel Morskie Oko (100 beds) Avenue Krupowki 30.

In 1st Category Pensions. Pensjonat Swiatomir (84 beds) Avenue Zeromskiego 17. Phone 26-49.

In 2nd Category Pensions. Pensjonat Lipowy (78 beds) Avenue Tetmajera 28b. Phone 28-28.

Pensjonat Teresa (22 beds) Avenue B. Czecha 6a. Phone 28-49.

Pensjonat Szopenowka (39 beds) Avenue Jagiellonska 18. Phone 22-23.

Pensjonat Bazumi (10 beds) Antalowka 8. Phone 38-45.

Pensjonat Smerekow (17 beds) Avenue Piaseckiego. Phone 21-22.

(3) *Hotels Outside Zakopane*

At Polana Chocholowska. PTTK Hostel Schronisko (200 beds). Phone 24-64.

(4) *Restaurants*

Hotel Giewont. Avenue Kosciuszki 1. (Dancing).
Watra. Avenue Zamojskiego 2. (Dancing).
Jedrus. Avenue Swierczewskiego 5. (Dancing).
Wierchy. Avenue Tetmajera 2. (Dancing).
Morskie Oko. Avenue Krupowki (Dancing).
Dom Turysty. Avenue Zaruskiego 5. (Dancing).

(5) *Cafés*

Hotel Giewont. Avenue Kosciuszki 1. (Music).
Europejska. Avenue Krupowki 27. (Also has a garden).

(6) *Museums*

Tatras Regional Museum. Avenue Krupowki 10.

(7) *Cinemas*

Morskie Oko. Avenue Krupowki.
Giewont. Place Zwyciestwa.

(8) *Orbis*

The Orbis travel and currency exchange office is at Avenue Krupowki.

THE SUDETEN MOUNTAINS

South of Wroclaw towards the Czech border are the Sudeten mountains which cover an area of about two hundred square miles.

Though in places they do rise to more than 3,000 feet they are characterised by their gentler contours with spruce forests and tiny lakes although in some spots you will find rocky outcrops and small gorges.

The trouble with these mountains is that they do tend to be windswept and in places seem very much like our own moorlands. Popular with people from the nearby Silesian mining and industrial centres, they are somewhat away from the main international tourist track.

A good stepping-off point for this area is the small town of *Walbrzych* which has three tourist hotels—the Dom Turysty with 145 beds, the Grunwald with 151 beds and the Dom Wycieczkowy with 52 beds.

PART VII

POLAND'S AMBER COAST

GDAŃSK

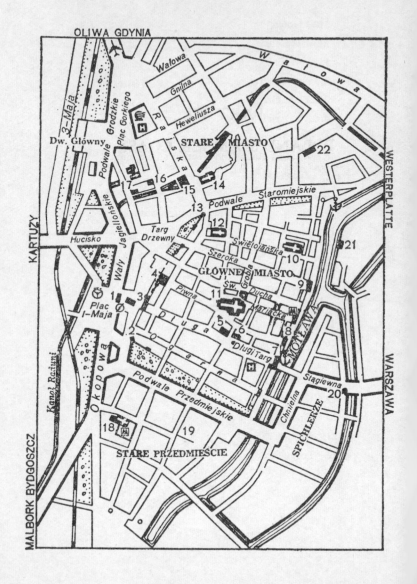

OLIWA GDYNIA

Wałowa

Gnilna

Heweliusza

3-Maja

Dw. Główny

Plac Gorkiego

Grodzkie

Rajska

Podwale

STARE   MIASTO

22

17   16

15   14

13   Podwale   Staromiejskie

KARTUZY

Jagiellońskie

Targ
Drzewny

12

Świętojańska

10

21

Hucisko

Wały

Szeroka

GŁÓWNE   MIASTO

9

Piwna

11   Św. Ducha

4

Grobla

1   3

Plac
I-Maja

2

Kanał Raduni

Długa

Mariacka

8

5   6

MOTŁAWA

Długi Targ   7

Okopowa

Podwale   Przedmiejskie

Stągiewna

20

Chmielna

18   19

SPICHLERZE

STARE PRZEDMIEŚCIE

MALBORK BYDGOSZCZ

WESTERPLATTE

WARSZAWA

KEY TO THE GDANSK MAP

H = Hotels

M = Museums

1. Wyzynna Gate
2. Narozna Tower
3. Zlota Gate
4. The Armoury
5. The Town Hall
6. Arthur's House and Neptune's Fountain
7. Zielona Gate
8. St. Mary's Gate
9. Old Crane and Archaeological Musuem
10. St. John's Church
11. St. Mary's Church
12. St. Nicholas' Church
13. Jacek Tower
14. St. Catherine's Church
15. Great Mill
16. Old Town Hall
17. St. Joseph's Church
18. Holy Trinity Church
19. Church of SS. Peter and Paul
20. Granary Island
21. Royal Granary
22. Post Office

POLAND'S AMBER COAST

The Poles are proud of their Baltic Coast. It is not overlong as coastlines go. No more than 365 miles separates Szczecin in the west from Braniewo not far from the Soviet–Lithuanian border in the east.

What it lacks in length is certainly compensated in interest and beauty. Much of Poland's turbulent history is bound up in her struggles to maintain an outlet to the sea—a struggle which eventually engulfed the world when the political problem of the 'Polish Corridor' became the running fuse to World War II.

The colours of Poland's coasts are silver-gold sand, soft woodland greens with the Baltic's pale translucent blues. Together they make up enchanted miles of seashore to which the Poles in their thousands flock from June to early September turning vast stretches of sand into noisy, happy-go-lucky pleasure beaches, though we found it easy to discover deserted beaches which we shared with a few sea-birds.

Around Gdansk and Sopot the shore is backed by promenades, formal gardens, houses, holiday villas and hotels, but moving westward the scene changes. Buildings begin to thin out and disappear and the soft silver gold sand takes over. Sandbars trap water to form inland lakes and lagoons, playgrounds for yachtsmen and small boat enthusiasts who prefer the calm quiet waters to the more restless sea seen across the sandbanks.

At Leba the sands assume the proportions of a small desert which in the winter gales moves to strangle the pines which form a background along this shore. Some of the dunes held by coarse grass are 300 feet high.

21. Gdansk Arthur's House with the Neptune Fountain

22. Gdansk— the Neptune Fountain

23. The Castle at Malbork

24. The Knights' Hall at Malbork Castle

If you stray away from the sea shore you are in a country of meadows, rivers, woods, forests and low green hills, pleasant rather than spectacular countryside, but dotted with some of Poland's more historic towns.

The twenty-two mile long Hel peninsula, never more than a quarter of a mile wide, is fringed on both sides with beaches for which the word fabulous seems inadequate. They were some of the best beaches seen on our European travels, clean and uncluttered. Behind them were shady pine woods while the whole peninsula seemed full of small fishing villages, and bathing resorts with odd names like Chalupy, Kuznica, Jastarnia, Jurata, not forgetting Hel itself which is at the tip of this long sandspit. At week-ends when trippers from Gdynia and Gdansk, which are just across the bay, arrive by boat the whole peninsula is quite lively with some of Poland's handsomest men and most beautiful girls sunning themselves on the beaches while children search the sands for the amber which can be picked up here, especially after a storm, though it is more frequently found on the less popular beaches of Leba, Darlowo and Ustka.

Our two most vivid memories of Poland's beaches are of the beach-clad Poles and their great basket chairs.

Stripped for bathing the average Pole though slightly stocky is admirably proportioned, while the women seem to carry their elegance even to the way they wear their bathing costumes and bikinis. We cannot recall having seen one obese Pole, either male or female, on any bathing beach or town visited. They are a handsome race of people seen at their best on the Baltic beaches.

We also took to the vast hooded wickerwork beach chairs which shielded us from the wind and could quite easily be turned to face the sun. There are no serried lines of bathing huts and deck chairs anywhere.

Another great advantage of these chairs is that they do give a great degree of privacy when going through the contortions of putting on and stripping off swimwear.

Though a few young Poles did carry transistor radios to the beach, these were too few to be regarded as a menace, and as most Polish youngsters prefer to swim and play beach games rather than loll about we hardly noticed they had transistor radios until they passed close by.

GDANSK

Gdansk is perhaps better known by its German name of Danzig. It is an ideal centre from which to visit Poland's Baltic playground. In its own right it is a city which deserves to be seen and you should allow yourself plenty of time to browse through its narrow streets and alleys when you have finished seeing its more noteworthy sights.

One of Poland's oldest cities, mentioned as far back as A.D. 997 and in a Papal Bull of 1148, in 1308 it was captured by the Teutonic Knights who butchered 10,000 citizens, burned the town and destroyed its fortifications. Shortly afterwards they built a castle, replanned the defences, resettling the city with Germans whose descendants triggered off the most destructive of world wars.

During the Renaissance, Danzig, a member of the Hanseatic League, was one of Europe's great trading ports. Her most outstanding monuments were built during this period.

The discovery of America and the shift in trade routes to the ports of Europe's western seaboard followed by the destructive Swedish Wars destroyed Danzig's economic importance. Annexed in the eighteenth century by Prussia it was held by Germany until the end of the First World War. During this period Danzig was thoroughly Germanised as part of German policy.

The Treaty of Versailles made Danzig a Free City under the control of the League of Nations. In case of war Poland was made responsible for its defence, and in what was a demilitarised city was allowed a small defensive arsenal.

Poland also had one official representative to speak for Danzig in international affairs, but he was hampered by a Town Council predominantly Nazi who wanted re-unification with Germany.

Though Danzig was Poland's main port her position was so difficult politically that she began to develop Gdynia a small fishing town fourteen miles north of Danzig. Although Danzig lost much trade to Gdynia the Poles did support Danzig's efforts to modernise her port facilities.

With the coming of Hitler, Danzig's German population increased their agitation for re-unification. Hitler supported them and Danzig soon became a major European political headache.

The Czechoslovakian problem resolved by appeasement, Danzig quickly became Europe's Number One trouble spot. But this problem was not to be solved so easily. In solving it thirty million people died, Danzig and most of Poland, much of Europe, North Africa and some of the Far East lay in ruins.

It was on September 1st 1939 when the small Polish garrison at Westerplatte just outside the city were attacked that the first shots of World War II were fired. When liberated on March 30th 1945, Danzig was in ruins, the harbour devastated, its basin filled with sunken ships.

Danzig, incorporated into the New Poland with its name changed to Gdansk, immediately began the work of reconstruction. As in Warsaw and so many other Polish war-devastated cities the pattern of rebuilding was to re-create the old so that future generations would be able to benefit from Poland's cultural heritage. When that had been successfully accomplished Gdansk was encompassed by new architecture.

The road into Gdansk is across flat country laced with small rivers and dykes. It is a good road built by gangs of war prisoners, including British, who lived in the numerous prison camps which covered this area.

If you arrive at the main station by train from Poznan or Warsaw, you will be able to step almost into the Old City, the *Royal Road* or Krolewska Droga comprising Dluga and Dlugi Targ Streets starting almost in front of the railway station, or at least after a very short walk along Jagiellonskie Street.

Although most streets in the older part of the city are charming, this is the most interesting of the city's streets though 90 per cent was totally destroyed and what you now see is no more than a painstaking reconstruction.

The Royal Road begins and ends with gates; at the top end is the *Brama Wyzynna* or High Gate and at the other end when it reaches the Motlawa River is the *Zielona Brama* or Green Gate.

The Brama Wyzynna was part of the original fortifications and like much of Gdansk was originally built by William van den Blocke, a Dutch architect who with his compatriot Antoine van Opbergen during the sixteenth century built many merchants' houses and public buildings. This particular gate was the main city gate and built into the ramparts which were protected by wide moats. The ramparts and the moats have gone, and only this portal with the Polish, Prussian and Gdansk coats of arms above its archway remains.

The red brick tower with a rather distinctive roof which stands just behind the Brama Wyzynna was also part of the fortifications. This was a prison and torture chamber though its main role was to protect the *Zlota Brama* or the inner gate leading to Dluga Street and the city.

At the start of *Dluga Street* is the *Dwor Bractwa Sw. Jerzego* a beautiful late Gothic building. Headquarters of a sixteenth century citizens' order of riflemen, the building has a small tower capped by a large metal statue of St. George slaying the dragon. In fact the words Sw. Jerzego are the Polish spelling of St. George.

Dluga Street is in two parts—that known as Dluga Street being slightly narrower than its continuation Dlugi Targ with the small Rynek or market place just past the Town Hall being the dividing mark.

The whole street is lined with old reconstructed merchants' houses, with tall gables, large airy windows, rich ornamentation—some picked out in gold—lamps hanging in beautiful wrought iron baskets and with fronts colourwashed in ochre, green and gold. The effect is wonderful and makes you realise how much wealth must have flowed into seventeenth century Gdansk to make all this possible.

Midway along Dluga Street just before you reach the Dlugi Targ or Long Market is the old *Town Hall* its lower half built in the fourteenth century. But it is the 270 feet high tower which catches the eye, an enormous sixteenth century clock face breaking its severity. Above the clock are balconies after which the tower becomes more fanciful with tiny turrets and little gilded flags ending in a slender cupola topped off with a gilded statue of King Sigismund Augustus. The tower has something of the attraction of the Hôtel de Ville in Brussels but it does not have a large fronting square to set it off properly.

Beyond the Town Hall is the loveliest part of Dluga Street, small trees making the perfect frame for the enchanting *Neptune Fountain* backed by the *Dwor Artusa* or Arthur's house.

The fountain is really beautiful. Above the circular bowl Neptune, his legs wrapped around by a fish's tail, stands poised with downward pointing trident. Cast in 1615 it is surrounded by a glorious seventeenth century grille ornamented with great gilt Polish eagles. Water spouts from the horn held in his hand and from the bowl's elevated rim.

But much of the attraction of the Neptune Fountain is due to the wonderful background afforded by the Dwor Artusa with its white stonework broken by great arched windows stretching almost from street to second storey level, the whole finished off by balconies and a low upper storey with niched statues and airy windows. With long shallow steps leading to an elaborately carved doorway it is a lovely building.

This is the *Rynek* or market place where public executions used to take place right up to the nineteenth century. The Gdansk citizens living in these lovely houses must have envied their good fortune for executions were regarded as public spectacles to be enjoyed.

After passing the gilded majesty of what is known as the *Golden Mansion* the Royal Road ends at the sixteenth century *Zielona Brama* or Green Gate whose archway leads you on to a bridge across the Motlawa River. After the gilt and glory of the Royal Road this all seems a bit grey with the quays and boats on a turgid yellow river.

But it was along this river that the wealth of sixteenth

and seventeenth century Gdansk flowed. On the *Spichlerze Island*—Granary Island—reached by crossing the bridge, two hundred big grain warehouses were built and protected by the strong defence towers which you can still see.

Take a walk along the *Moltawa Quays* but don't get too interested in the river or you will do as we almost did and overlook the old gateways which could at night and in times of war shut off all the side streets making the city well-nigh impregnable. But as we were already interested in the great bulk of the *Zuraw Gdanski* which had figured on so many souvenirs offered for sale in the shops, perhaps we should be forgiven.

Built in 1444 the Zuraw Gdanski has, after being a war casualty, been rebuilt. It not only served as a medieval crane, its huge hoists landing cargo and fitting ships' masts, but it was part of the Gdansk defence system, its fortified gateways being the entrance into the old city.

With its great wooden hoist tower jutting above the river you certainly won't miss it and it is certainly worth walking down to see.

Retrace your steps and take the gateway into *Mariacka Street* which is also lined with some reconstructed sixteenth century houses especially that next to the *Nadwodna Gate*. Kept clean and tidy, this is another delightful corner of the old city.

Mariacka Street ends in a small square behind the choir of *St. Mary's Church*, sometimes known as the *Church of Our Lady of Gdansk* which not only dominates the city but is Poland's largest Gothic church and one of Europe's biggest. Begun in 1343 and finished in 1502 it is 340 feet in length, 88 feet in height with a 245 foot tower. Built in a cruciform shape it can seat 25,000 people. Like most of Gdansk it was a war casualty being bombed, shelled and burnt, but with government aid it has been completely restored.

We are not impressed by size and this vast red brick church was certainly not our 'cup of tea'. The great tower is far too bulky and seen with the slender soaring pinnacle of the Town Hall on the same skyline looks too heavy. But being only an average tourist and not an architect, my idea of what makes a good building might well be wrong.

Its interior is quite simple, a nave, two aisles, some vaulting supported on tall pillars with beautifully decorated capitals. There are side chapels, one with the fifteenth century statue of the Madonna, which with a few tombs, the 'Last Judgement' by the Flemish artist Memling and a mediaeval altar, is about all that was saved from the war.

Close by the great church is the tiny baroque *Royal Chapel* (Kaplica Krolewska) built in 1678 at the request of King John Sobieski III.

To get back to the station and the Orbis hotel from St. Mary's Church take a walk along *Piwna Street*. This is yet another street which has had a post-war face lift though the merchants' houses are not quite so grand as those along the Dluga. Their colour-washed fronts, fine gables and large windows, the bulk of St. Mary's Church shutting off one end of the street, looked quite like old Amsterdam.

At the west end of Piwna Street is the old *arsenal* built in 1605. With its shopping arcade and its brick and sandstone front richly decorated and traces of old fortifications it is one of the more interesting city buildings.

We have only touched on a few places worth seeing in the old part of the city—but as in Warsaw, to get the feel of the place you must explore it on foot, you will hardly want to try the trams packed tight with strap hangers overspilling on to the steps and clinging in limpet fashion to the sides.

You will find plenty of good shops, bars, cafés and restaurants. The people of Gdansk are well dressed though the women are not so elegant as those of Warsaw and the men more heavily built. In fact there is still something of a Germanic air about the place and German seems almost as widely spoken as Polish.

If you have time take one of the steamers from the landing stage near the Zielona Brama for a short tour around the port or downstream to Sopot. The longer trip passes the tiny fortress of *Westerplatte* whose garrison of 182 soldiers from 1st–7th September 1939 withstood bombing and shelling as they fought the Wehrmacht, only capitulating when they knew most of Poland had been over-run and further resistance futile.

Another short worthwhile trip is to *Oliwa* a city suburb which not only has a fine eighteenth century park and rock garden with high clipped hedges overlooking an ornamental lake with swans, but a *cathedral* with an interesting organ of 6,000 pipes which plays music, shakes the cathedral, produces a loud echo and causes figures of angels to blow trumpets or ring tiny bells while models of the sun and stars revolve. Quite a remarkable tourist sight which usually happens at noon or at any other time if you pay a nominal charge.

When the organ was built in the eighteenth century seven men pumped the bellows. Today pumping is done electrically. Though the cathedral has other worthwhile things to see including some paintings the organ is its great attraction.

You can combine a visit to Oliwa—easily reached by tram or bus from the city centre—with a swim from one of Gdansk's bathing beaches at Stogi, Brzelno or

Jelitkowo, though when we went you could hardly see the sand for people.

We spent a very pleasant evening strolling in Gdansk's old city streets. In the Baltic's strange white evening light they took on a new beauty, the bases of the houses lost in shadows, fanciful gables outlined against a pearl grey sky, soft lights shining in tiny shop windows. There was little neon to destroy the illusion of being in another age. In fact the absence of over-large neon signs is a Polish feature which gets our strongest approval, so do the gay little clubs of Gdansk where you can pass pleasant hours drinking, chatting and watching people dance on pocket handkerchief sized floors. Make a point of watching Polish men take their partners on to the dance floor. Before beginning to dance they press the lady's hand to their lips and do the same when the band stops. It's all very romantic. Carried out by men less tough and virile than the Poles it would appear sloppy.

INFORMATION FOR THOSE PLANNING TO STAY IN GDANSK

(1) *How to Get There*

By through international express trains from Ostend or the Hook of Holland to Poznan then by fast local trains. There are coach links from Warsaw and Poznan while LOT operate direct domestic flights from Warsaw to Gdansk.

(2) *Hotels*

In 1st Class Category. Orbis Hotel Monopol (197 beds) Gorkiego Square 1. Phone 31-68-51.

Hotel Turystyczny (41 beds) Avenue Heweliusza 6.

In 2nd Class Category. Dom Wycieczkowy (62 beds) Dluga Street 45. Phone 31-25-69.

In 3rd Class Category. Hotel Dworcowy (25 beds) Avenue Brzozowa 5. Phone 41-24-03.

(3) *Private Accommodation*

Accommodation in private houses in Gdansk and in Holiday Chalets at the beach resorts of Gdansk-Stogi and Gdansk-Jelitkowo can be obtained through the 'Balt-Tourist' Accommodation Bureau, 3, Karmelicka Street, Gdansk. Phone 31-38-74.

(4) *Restaurants*

If you like dancing with your meals try the Cristal in Grunwaldzka Street near the large PDT Departmental Store the Gedania at Dluga Street 75; Jantar, Dlugi Targ 18; the Kameleon at Armis Radzieckiej Street 18 at Gdansk-Oliwa is a good out-of-city choice.

(5) *Cafés*

Marysienka—Szercka Street 29 has dancing; Kameralna, Dluga Street 37 and the Morska, Grunwaldzka Street 45 have music.

(6) *Museums*

Archaeological Museum, 25/26 Mariacka Street.
Maritime Museum, 67/68 Szeroka Street.
Pomeranian Museum, 25, Rzelnicka Street.

(7) *Shopping*

Gdansk has some good shops. Visit the Departmental Store PDT at Grunwaldzka Street 56. Handicraft and Folk Art souvenirs can be bought at the Ceplia Shops at Dluga Street 47/49 or Grunwaldzka 31.

(8) *Theatres*

Lalki, Aktora Avenue 1.
Miniatura, Grunwaldzka 16.
Latek, Garncarska 18/20.
Wybrzeze, Zwyciestwa Avenue 15.

(9) *Cinemas*

Bajka, Jaskowa Dolnia 44.
Kameralne, Dluga Street 57.
Leningrad, Dluga Street 57.

(10) *Orbis*

The Orbis exchange and travel office is at 1, Gorkiego Square.

(11) *Steamer Excursions*

These can be booked at Grodzka Street 17 or at the landing stages at Zielona Brama and at Wartka Street.

(12) *Information*

For general information on Gdansk and district write to: Provincial Tourist Information Centre Gdansk, 10/11, Elzbietanska Street. Phone 31-38-74.

SOPOT

Seven miles to the north, Sopot can be easily reached by train, bus or steamer from Gdansk.

We drove out passing the new Oliwa residential area with its ten-storeyed blocks of flats. It was a fairly busy road, heavy lorries on their way to the factories and port of Gdynia mixing with the pleasure traffic, though the volume was light compared with other countries, most Poles still having to rely on public transport.

Sopot was bigger than we had imagined. Maybe the resort photos we had seen with the green hills in the background had created a false impression—but though it began life as a spa way back in the seventeenth century, it is only in the last fifty years that it has grown to any size (population 45,000) to become not only the most popular of Polish bathing resorts but the undisputed rival of the German pleasure beaches at Travemünde and Warnemünde.

We found the beach excellent—a wide stretch of soft silver gold sand sloping almost imperceptibly making it suitable for non-swimmers and small children. Despite the crowds—there must have been at least five thousand people spread on a mile of shore—the sands were surprisingly clean. The Poles are a tidy people. You never see them throwing match sticks or sweet papers down and when they moved away they made certain that they left the beach tidy.

Though there were a few deck and basket chairs to be seen the majority of people were content to enjoy the clear, surprisingly warm September sunshine, by stretching out on a towel.

Immediately behind the beach is a made-up promenade and a park of neatly clipped privet hedges where people walked and sat in the sun.

One of the things we liked about Sopot was the amount of greenery. In places the trees came right down to the beach. Villas and hotels were set among trees and gardens while the low tree-clad hills rising behind the town added to the impression of a garden city.

Sopot is proud of its pier which is about six hundred yards long and quite wide. There is no pier toll so you can stroll along it to sit in the sun on one of its many seats. At the end of the pier you will find the landing bays for the passenger steamers to and from Gdansk and Gdynia. Here you board the steamers to cross the yacht-dotted Gulf of Gdansk to Hel and Jastarnia on the peninsula.

Next to the pier is the Orbis Grand Hotel with its green copper cupola, tree-shaded terrace and small private beach. We lunched here in a setting of Edwardian splendour which somehow recaptured the inter-war years when large numbers of Central Europe's aristocracy flocked here. Now it is filled with quite a different type of tourist.

Sopot's main thoroughfares are the Grundwaldzka and Powstancow Warszawy Streets which run behind and parallel to the promenade and beach, and the Bohaterow Monte Cassino from the railway station through the town to the pier.

At its north end, along the Avenue Sepia we discovered a well laid out camping site, while behind the railway station the Avenue Moniuszki reached along the Podjazd took us into the hills where there is a horse racing track.

In the hills and also reached along Moniuszki Avenue you will find the celebrated *Open Air Theatre* (Opera Lesna) which can seat five thousand people spread on tiers rising above the stage. Very much like the Greek Theatre at Epidaurus but of course the setting is greener though the acoustics are equally good.

There is plenty of life in Sopot. The cafés were full. There was music for dancing, and though Viennese Waltzes, Tangos and Fox Trots were popular with people of all ages, when the bands played the Twist the floors became crowded. We also saw signs of the 'rhythm and blues' and other get-with-it dances.

All the main streets had their selection of souvenir and other shops. There were ice cream and soft drink stands, kiosks selling everything from cigarettes to postage stamps, in fact it was a typical beach resort of the more popular kind where you could spend two weeks pleasantly if you wanted no more from your holiday than a good beach, a comfortable bed, some night life and coach excursions.

(1) *How to Get There*

By through express trains from Ostend or the Hook of Holland to Poznan, then by fast local trains via Gdansk. There are also coach services from Poznan and Warsaw. Those wishing to fly can book to Gdansk airport and continue by road.

(2) *Hotels*

In S Category. Grand Hotel (236 beds) Avenue Powstancow Warszawy 8/12. Phone 51-16-52.

In 2nd Class Category. Hotel Wanda (58 beds) Avenue Poniatowskiego 7. Phone 51-18-96.

Hotel Bungalow (52 beds) Avenue Sepia 50. Phone 51-14-30.

Hotel Wiktor (50 beds) Avenue Kosciuszki 47. Phone 51-17-71.

In 2nd Class Tourist Category. Dom Turysty (358 beds) Avenue Sepia 51. Phone 51-14-58.

(3) *Private Accommodation*

Accommodation in private houses can be reserved by writing to the Biuro Zakwaterowan, 4 Dworcowa Street. Phone 5-26-17.

(4) *Holiday Chalets*

There is an establishment renting holiday chalet accommodation at 51, Bitwy Pod Plowcami Street. Phone 5-30-77.

(5) *Camping*

There is an excellent camping site by the Dom Turysty, Avenue Sepia 51.

(6) *Restaurants*

Ermital, 23 Bohaterow Monte Cassino (Dancing).
Grand Hotel, Avenue Powstancow Warszawy (Dancing).

(7) *Cafés*

You will find several good ones with music and dancing close to the pier.

(8) *Shopping*

Most of your shopping can be done along the Bohaterow Monte Cassino where you will find department stores as well as souvenir shops.

(9) *Orbis*

The Orbis office for booking excursions and changing your money can be found at Bohaterow Monte Cassino 33.

(10) *Information*

You can get a lot of local information including programmes of local events by calling at the PTTK Information Centre Sopot, 12, Konstytucji 3 Maja Square. Phone 5-12-68.

GDYNIA

From Sopot we continued by way of Orlowo to Gdynia which lies below the *Kepa Redlowska*, a tree-covered hill which in one direction falls steeply to the sea, in the other to the centre of Gdynia.

On the summit of the hill we enjoyed a fine view of the town with the modern housing estates sweeping down towards the harbour, where a forest of cranes worked on the many vessels packing the port.

Though Gdynia has a population of 169,000 its interest lies in its phenomenal development.

In 1923 Gdynia was no more than a small fishing port of less than 1,000 people. When Gdansk became a Free Port and Poland after a century of isolation from the Baltic obtained her narrow corridor to the sea, it was essential for her to build a port if she was to develop a world trade. Gdynia was the obvious and only spot.

No sooner had Gdynia been transferred to Poland than work began. The Poles, normally a hard-working people, set about their task with typical speed and thoroughness, startling the western world which so often spends years discussing plans of this dimension before daring to begin work.

The Poles took sixteen years to change a sleepy fishing town of less than 1,000 inhabitants into a world port with six miles of quays, warehouses, refrigeration sheds, a rice-husking mill, an oil refinery, a dry dock and homes for a population of 130,000 people—a port which, much to the fury of Hitler, drew shipping tonnage away from Danzig (Gdansk) and Stettin (Szczecin). Gdynia's growth as much as anything else kept the 'Polish Question' on the hob and eventually helped to precipitate World War II.

Badly damaged during the early part of the War, Gdynia felt the full fury of the Nazis during their 1945 retreat from the combined Polish-Russian army. The quays, warehouses, cranes and breakwater were dynamited and reduced to rubble. The battleship *Gneisenau* was scuttled to block the harbour entrance. Apart from a swollen population living in war-battered homes Gdynia was back where she started.

Today, as you stand on the heights of the Kepa Redlowska looking at the busy city stretched out below, you, even though there are some open spaces where rebuilding has yet to be completed, you realise that Gdynia is fully functioning with the most vital of her war damage mended. It is yet another Polish post-war miracle. That alone makes a fleeting glimpse of Gdynia worthwhile.

MALBORK

To visit the Baltic Coast and not see Malbork Castle would be a great pity for it is one of Poland's great tourist treasures.

It is only thirty-five miles by road from Gdansk to Malbork, a run through flat country with high river banks reminding you that you are on the Vistula delta.

We crossed the river at Knibawa and shortly after to our left saw the immense pile of Malbork rising above the rich flat farmland.

Built in the late thirteenth century by the Teutonic Knights, the castle was not only the most powerful unit in their system of strong points, but one of Europe's strongest castles surrounded by a double circle of walls strengthened by towers and strong points.

The part of the castle which from the distance first catches your eye is the keep, or as the guide was later to call it, the High Castle, its oldest portion. In addition to the keep there is the Middle Castle, three-winged and built around a spacious courtyard, the whole enclosed by double defence walls and a moat.

We crossed the moat by a covered wooden footbridge which took us under the massive defence gate into the Middle Castle courtyard. Large and full of light it is surrounded by strong Gothic buildings with narrow windows for defence and to let in the light.

The guide then took us into the refectory, an enormous vaulted hall whose roof is supported on three slender columns. It has a huge fireplace which gave some warmth in the bitter Polish winters but to us seemed less satisfactory than the beautiful stoves of Wawel and Nieborow. This was where the knights gathered to feast before setting out to battle. Their feasts were so celebrated that records show that knights and their ladies travelled across Europe to take part in them.

From the refectory hall a narrow stairway leads to the apartments of the Grand Master of the Teutonic Order and to the chapel with its fourteenth century murals showing incidents in the lives of St. Peter and St. Paul. From the chapel you pass into the two halls where the Grand Master held court. Traceried windows let in sufficient light to enable you to admire the vaulted Gothic ceiling held by one slender column.

To reach the High Castle we crossed another bridge spanning a sixty-foot deep moat and walked along a cobbled passageway under the vaulting of the great defence gates.

We were now in the smaller and darker High Castle courtyard with arcades running all around it and on first floor level lovely, late Gothic traceried windows. It was far more beautiful than the courtyard we had just left.

In its centre is a deep well covered by a steep pantiled roof surmounted by a carved pelican. A massive wooden wheel was used to help those drawing water.

A wide stone staircase took us to the first floor where we encircled the building looking on to the courtyard through the traceried cloister windows. We went into the domed Chapter built in 1310, walked along a covered passage into the Gdansk Tower which looked out to the River Nogent and the countryside beyond and admired the twelfth century 'Golden Gate' with its ten gold figures of women.

211

Hours can be spent in Malbork walking along the ramparts, inspecting the kitchens, dungeons, sleeping quarters, courtyards and gateways which together form this mighty but magnificent structure.

The castle was severely damaged by the Nazis in their 1945 retreat but following the liberation it was slowly and painstakingly restored.

Malbork town has not been quite so lucky having been almost entirely destroyed. Only fragments remain of the massive fourteenth century defence walls with their thirteen bastions and two defence gates though the fourteenth century *Town Hall* and the fifteenth century *St. John's Church* are more or less intact.

During the war many prisoner of war camps were set up around Malbork, the men working on road repair and construction. To the south of the town on the Sztum road is a small *British and American cemetery*. There is also a Russian cemetery for those who died fighting to liberate Malbork.

The cemeteries are beautifully kept with a memorial stone to commemorate the young men who died so far from home in this flat, still countryside.

If you wish to stay over in Malbork you will find two 3rd Class Category hotels: the Miejski (64 beds) in Kosciuszki Street and the Dom Wycieczkowy (81 beds) in Hibnera Street in the shadow of the mighty fortress.

A popular day trip from Gdansk, Sopot and Gdynia, Malbork has restaurants, cafés and a sizable coach and car park.

SZCZECIN

To the west, almost on the border with East Germany is Szczecin, perhaps more widely known by its German name of Stettin, an important Polish seaport and industrial centre with a population of around 270,000.

The town has had a chequered history. Starting out as a Polish city in the thirteenth century it was infiltrated by German settlers who established Szczecin as an important Baltic trading port, which in 1360 with other Polish cities joined the Hanseatic League.

Although during the Reformation Szczecin became Protestant and often suffered during the wars which swept across this corner of Poland, the city flourished.

In 1637 by the Treaty of Westphalia, Szczecin was acquired by Sweden, but less than a hundred years later it was sold to the Prussians who as part of their policy of complete Germanisation changed its name to Stettin.

Because it is close to Berlin, under German rule the city and port grew to become the Baltic's biggest port. Though Poles continued to live in Szczecin they did in fact become a minority and in a population of a quarter of a million only ten thousand were Poles though they tenaciously clung to their ancient culture and ways of life and even had their own schools.

The last war dealt harshly with Szczecin. Most of the port and city were destroyed by the Allied air attacks of 1943 while the fierce fighting which took place during the 1945 Soviet break-through completed the damage.

After the war Szczecin was given back to Poland who began the task of rebuilding the city, quickly regaining a great deal of her former trade even though Germany is politically divided.

If you are passing through, you will find Szczecin still has several interesting monuments, the Old Town starting quite close to the railway station.

The eighteenth century *Brama Portowa* or Sea Gate with its rather fanciful sculptures catches the eye, so does the tower of *St. James' Church. St. John's Church* at the end of Wielka Street overlooking the River Oder is undoubtedly the city show-piece. Built in the thirteenth century it escaped most of the damage and that done has been skilfully restored.

The war totally destroyed the old market place—*Rynek Stary*—which opens on to the river, only fragments of the *Town Hall* and the *Loytz Palace* remained. Research in Polish archives and painstaking re-building have produced fine replicas of the originals.

Close to the old market and set on a low hill is the *Zamek* or town castle which having been built in the fourteenth century for city defence was in the nineteenth century turned into an office and shopping block and then as part of a city rebuilding plan by Haussmann who designed modern Paris, it was almost levelled, only part of the lower floors, crypt and cellars remaining.

Most of the castle seen today, its fanciful gables covered in part by creepers, is a replica though the tombs of the Pomeranian Dukes seen in the crypt are the originals.

Szczecin is a very pleasant town, with broad tree-lined boulevards radiating from the many city squares. You will find good shops, restaurants, cinemas, theatres —in fact it is very much the prosperous busy commercial city.

Tucked away from the main tourist circuits, unless you have a specific reason for wanting to go there, it could well be omitted from your holiday itinerary.

It is worth remembering that Szczecin is only twenty miles from the Baltic coast and close to some bathing resorts such as *Trzebiz* which has a beautiful beach, *Nowe Warpno* and *Podgrodzie* which is a family resort, the beach being especially suited to small children.

INFORMATION FOR THOSE PLANNING TO STAY IN
SZCZECIN

(1) *How to Get There*

By train from Ostend or the Hook of Holland to
Poznan and then by local train. There are coach
connections by road from Poznan and Warsaw as well
as domestic air services both from Warsaw and Poznan
to Szczecin.

(2) *Hotels*

In S Category. Hotel Continental (105 beds) 3 Maja
Street 1. Phone 45-51.

In 1st Class Category. Hotel Piast (150 beds) Zwyciestwa Square 3.

Hotel Gryf (121 beds) Avenue W. Polskiego 49.
Phone 340-35.

Hotel Pomorski (91 beds) Brama Portowa 4. Phone
370-65.

In 2nd Class Category. Dom Turysty (182 beds)
Batorego Square 2. Phone 458-33.

Hotel Wielkopolanka (73 beds) Slaska Street 43.
Phone 462-42.

In 3rd Class Category. Hotel Nadodrzanski (139 beds)
Kaszubska Street 13. Phone 473-48.

(3) *Restaurants*

Kameralna—Piastow Street 16 (Dancing).
Artystyczna—Piastow Street 1.

(4) *Shopping*

The main shopping thoroughfare is the Wojska
Polskiego where you can buy all your souvenirs.

(5) *Orbis*

The Orbis office and currency exchange bureau is at
Wojska Polskiego 1. Phone 451-54.

PART VIII

LAKES AND FORESTS

LAKES AND FORESTS

When you try to imagine Poland you think of it as forest country. You hardly imagine it to be lake country—yet Poland has no less than 9,296 lakes of which 2,000 are tucked away in her north-east corner in the area known as Mazuria, paradise for anyone who likes water sports whether bathing, boating, yachting, canoeing, water ski-ing or simply fishing.

But Mazuria is more than a glittering wonderland of water. It is forest country too, with pines, firs, silver birch and copper beeches sweeping down to the lake-sides. Some giant trees are hundreds of years old. In the thickets and sunny forest clearings you can surprise all kinds of wild life including herds of stag, roebuck, tiny wild horses locally known as Tarpans, an occasional wild boar, foxes, badgers and wolves.

Many lakes are joined by shallow meandering streams providing the canoeist with hours of sport. Some larger lakes have been linked by canals, but as in most countries these have long ceased to be of commercial use though we often saw pleasure craft filled with holidaymakers passing along them as they explored the lakes, as part of an organised day trip from one of the many holiday centres which have grown up in this area.

We were surprised by the clarity of many of the lakes enabling us to see objects lying on their beds as well as great shoals of fish.

The colourings were beautiful too. Sometimes the water appeared to be vivid blue, more often rich emerald and we also experienced some wonderful sunsets when the water turned to gold, orange and scarlet.

Some lakes were quite small, others vast inland seas with the shorelines stretching away to the horizon. Some of the larger lakes seemed to have floating islands similar to those we had seen in the Danube Delta on previous travels in Europe. These are formed by generations of dried and rotting plants which in time have sprouted young trees. When the wind catches their branches the vegetated islands on which they grow move across the water.

Quite a lot of what we thought was marshland turned out to be tiny lakes which are grown over, and unless you take care when walking you can have an unpleasant surprise though at the edges they are never deep.

The lakes provide homes for all kinds of water birds and we saw cormorants, swans, herons, cranes and tens of thousands of various species of wild duck. Polish fishermen told us that the lakes are full of pike, perch, bream, many reaching quite a large size and for anyone interested in angling there is some rare sport.

Throughout Mazuria the Poles have built little holiday villages where you can live in comfortable wooden bungalows, eating in the camp restaurants. For a small charge all kinds of water craft from sailing yachts to canoes can be hired, hire charges for a sailing yacht being around $3 a day.

Many of the holiday villages seemed to have their own bathing pools for those who are not enthusiastic about lake bathing. And most of them also seemed to organise a programme of sightseeing excursions as well as some kind of evening entertainment. Charges inclusive of all meals worked out about $3 per person per day which we thought to be cheap enough.

If you happen to be motoring through Poland en route to the Soviet Union, with a small detour you can see some of Poland's finest lakes and forests.

Leaving Warsaw motor eastwards in the direction of Brest Litovsk but at Siedlice turn north towards Bialystok. The distance is about 220 miles, the undulating countryside pleasant enough and more interesting than if you keep to the main highway through Ostrow.

At Siedlice (it has an eighteenth century palace, an old Town Hall and some textile factories) turn north to Sokolow Podlaski then east to Drohiczyn.

DROHICZYN

This is a pretty little town (population 2,000) situated on the high banks of the River Bug backed by its castle hill.

Local legend has it that every hundred years the hillside opens and boats filled with armed knights emerge to sail down the river, re-entering at dawn the hill which closes behind them.

At one time Drohiczyn was obviously of some importance, why else should so small a town have four rather lovely seventeenth century churches which are worth looking at.

SIEMIATYCZE

Siemiatycze is the next sizable place through which you will pass. There is nothing to hold you here, though by now you have left the main tourist routes and are receiving the special attentions given to such a rarity as a foreign traveller. Stop your car in any small village and see how quickly a crowd collects. Not necessarily to look at you but at your car which they will gently finger. Though the Poles manufacture a reasonably good car of their own—the Warsaw—the more exotic shapes of American and Western European cars act like a magnet even in large towns like Cracow and Lublin. You can imagine then the sensation they cause in the small towns and villages of Eastern Poland.

You can lunch at either Bielsk Podlaski or Hajnowka which will then give you most of the afternoon to see Bialowieza.

BIALOWIEZA

Leaving Hajnowka the road runs through thick woodlands. You are now on the perimeter of the great Bialowieza Forest, the largest in Europe covering almost 250,000 acres. Most of it is in the Soviet Union, the Polish–Soviet border following a wide riding track through the centre of the forest.

About 12,300 acres of the forest belong to Poland which has turned it into a National Park, which is well worth making a special journey to see as it is Europe's last virgin forest composed of fir trees growing to heights of 170 feet, 600 year old oaks almost as tall with trunks 6½ feet in diameter. There are pines, silver birch, lime trees, maples, elm and poplar mostly of great age and enormous size.

It is very hard to describe a great forest with the trees growing very close together, the lower half of their trunks devoid of leaves and branches which spread in canopies above. Where trees have fallen it is not unusual to find them being lodged against sturdier young ones. But perhaps it is the immense stillness of the forest which makes such an impression on you. We thought the forests of Poland beautiful.

Beautiful though the forests are, they are not the only reason to go to Bialowieza. The forest animals are just as interesting in particular the Zubr or Bison which in

222

Europe is only found at Bialowieza and in the Caucasus in South Russia.

The Bison of Bialowieza are larger than those of North America and through the centuries have been hunted by a long line of royal sportsmen as well as local poachers.

At the start of the first war in 1914 it was estimated that 200 Bison lived in the forest. After the war this number had been halved. The subsequent fighting between Poland and Russia which between 1918 and 1920 was through the forest killed off the few remaining Bison.

In 1930 the Polish Government contacted zoos and landowners in various parts of the world who had bred specimens of Polish Bison. As a result a few Bison were brought back to Bialowieza for breeding and by 1939 there was a small herd.

The last war and the hunting activities of Hermann Goering almost wiped them out again though sufficient remained to procreate under the protection of the Polish State who are said to have fed the survivors on vitamin pills. Today there are more than 100 Bison at Bialowieza, some running wild seeking out the lush grass, acorns and young tree shoots on which they feed, others at stud in a reservation with a diet supplemented by hay, oats and sugar beet.

All Bison born in the forest are given names beginning with letters such as PO, PL or KA.

But Bison are not the only forest animals at Bialowieza. There are stags, deer, lynx, wild boar, elk and tiny Tarpan horses. At one time bears could be seen snuffling around but they are now thought to have been exterminated. In the nineteenth century bee keeping was also a great forest industry, but it has died out completely though you can sometimes find a disused hive.

If you happen to like wild life and the great outdoors the Bialowieza Forest is treasure trove. On your forest walks you can study the insects, or watch the birds of which 200 different species have been recorded, while more than 1,000 different butterflies have been identified. I doubt whether there is any other area in Europe which can offer so much to interest the naturalist.

There is not much in Bialowieza village which is no more than a scattering of houses with a few small souvenir shops, cafés, one or two restaurants and a post office. Yet there always seems to be plenty of people carrying rucksacks, the men wearing tight knicker-bockers above bare legs with ankle socks and great boots, the women equally sturdy boots with stretch slacks, this seeming to be holiday uniform in most parts of rural Poland.

If you wish to stay over in Bialowieza you can get tourist accommodation at the Dom Wycieczkowy Hotel (175 beds) Park Narodowy. Phone 39.

To reach Bialystok some sixty miles north of Bia-lowieza you must drive back to Bielsk Podlaski and turn north to Zabludow, totally destroyed in the last war and ten miles from Bialystok.

Those without their own transport wishing to see Bialowieza can take the express from Warsaw (Dworzec Wilenski Station) to Bialystok and continue by slow train via Bielsk Podlaski.

BIALYSTOK

Bialystok (population 130,000) is the textile centre of north eastern Poland. Having been totally destroyed in the war, the town has been rebuilt and has little interest apart from the arcaded *Town Hall*, the *Church of St. Roch* with a 250-foot tower standing on a hill above the town

25. Bison in the Bialowieza Forest, Eastern Poland

26. One of the Mazurian Lakes

27. Gizycko Pier, in the Mazurian Lake district

28. The Palace at Lancut

and of modern design and the *Branicki Palace* which is the tourist attraction.

The Branicki Palace has been compared to Versailles though by no means as magnificent. Tylman van Gameren the Dutch architect who designed so many Polish palaces built Branicki somewhat after the style of Versailles with arcaded wings at each side of the main two-storeyed buildings flanked by towers.

Though the palace was damaged during the war and the Poles have gone to very great pains to restore it to its former glory it is of considerably less interest than other palaces such as Wilanow, Nieborow or Wawel, and the new apartment houses going up in the town spoiling the skyline behind the palace do not add to its attraction.

The park gateway, squat and whitewashed with a surprisingly graceful clock tower is very attractive, the park nice enough and the two large statues of Hercules in front of the palace eye-catching.

To us the main asset of Bialystok is its suitability as a touring centre from which to explore north-east Poland.

INFORMATION FOR THOSE PLANNING TO STAY AT BIALYSTOK

(1) *How to Get There*

There are express rail services from Warsaw direct to Bialystok, or you can travel by direct coach services leaving from the Warsaw Bus Station in Zytnia Street.

(2) *Hotels*

In *1st Class Category*. Hotel Cristal (250 beds) Avenue Lipowa 3. Phone 56-02.

H

(3) *Restaurants*

You will find several promising looking restaurants on the Sienkiewicza.

(4) *Orbis*

There is an Orbis office with currency exchange facilities at Rynek Kosciuszki 13.

From Bialystok you reach the Mazurian Lake District around Augustow by taking the secondary road to Knyszyn branching on to the side road to Korycin and going north to Suchowola in a wild countryside of forests, low hills and marshes which provide landscapes of sombre beauty.

AUGUSTOW

This small town (population 11,500) is a popular Mazurian holiday spot in what is considered one of the most beautiful parts of Poland. It is surrounded by some of the more attractive lakes including Sajno, Necko, and Bialy. Augustow with Suwalki twenty miles to the north between them share 450 lakes of varying size. Some lakes seemed to have quite high banks with tree-covered cliffs dropping down to the water. Some set in open valleys among the low hills were surrounded by meadows and farmland, others were almost hidden by deep forests awaiting discovery by those tourists prepared to follow forest paths to reach them.

East of the town you will find the Augustow Canal designed and built in the nineteenth century to link the River Niemen through the Mazurian Lakes with the Vistula and the port of Gdansk.

The canal is now only used to float logs to the sawmills and for pleasure trips.

The countryside around Augustow seemed to us to

hold some wonderful opportunities for fishing, boating, bathing and yachting. The walks beside the lakes or in the forests are numberless and there are organised excursions. Those interested in hunting have rare sport in the Augustow Forest with stag, wild boar and roebuck and among the birds the gaily hued capercaillie and wild duck. There is some night life in the town and plenty of souvenir shops.

INFORMATION FOR THOSE PLANNING TO STAY IN AUGUSTOW

(1) *How to Get There*

There is a reasonably good rail service from Warsaw through Bialystok and Elk also direct coach services.

(2) *Hotels*

In 1st Category Tourist. Hotel Dom Wyzieczkowy (140 beds) Augustow-Port. Phone 62.

In 3rd Class Category. Hotel Miejski, 36 Wojska Polskiego. Phone 86.

There are also two excellent tourist hostels in the area which are very popular with young people.

(3) *Restaurants*

You will find several good ones in Krasicki Square.

SUWALKI

Twenty miles north of Augustow, Suwalki is much larger and with a fine park in the town centre seemed a little more attractive though obviously not so popular mainly because the lakes are not quite so close to the town as at Augustow.

Lake Wigry seven miles to the south-east and reached by bus we thought particularly lovely with its wooded peninsulas pushing far into the lake and its little creeks and green islands. There are some lovely rivers too, especially the Czarna Hancza linking Lake Wigry with the Augustow Canal. Along this river, overhung in places by trees, you can glimpse interesting little villages with thatched roofs and beautifully carved doors and window frames.

Although on the quiet side, one of the joys of Suwalki was the total lack of international tourists who have yet to discover it, though there are always plenty of holiday-making Poles on its streets.

INFORMATION FOR THOSE PLANNING TO STAY AT SUWALKI

(1) *How to Get There*

By rail or bus from Warsaw.

(2) *Hotels*

In 3rd Class Category. Hotel Miejski (60 beds) Avenue Kosciuszki. Phone 64.

(3) *Restaurants*

There is a reasonably good restaurant at 75 Lenin Street.

(4) *Camping*

The Suwalki–Augustow Lake District offers some of Poland's very best camping facilities. Here are some of the camps open in the summer season:

Fracki—beautifully sited on the River Czarna Hanc-za. 15th June–15th September.

Gawrychruda—on Lake Wigry. July 1st–15th September.

Jalowy Rog—on the River Czarna Hancza. 15th June–15th September.

Kukle—on Lake Pomorze. 15th June–15th September.

Plaska—on the banks of the Augustow Canal. 15th June–15th September.

Serwy—on Lake Serwy. 15th June–15th September.

Stary Folwark—on Lake Wigry. It is attached to a tourist hostel. 1st June–30th September.

Swoboda and Studzieniczna—on Lake Studzieniczne. 15th June–15th September.

Wysoki Most—on the River Czarna Hancza. 1st July–15th September.

All the camps listed have facilities for providing full board and all are sited on the edge of the lakes, rivers or canals mentioned.

(5) *Loan Centre*

It is possible at surprisingly cheap cost to hire all kinds of camping and other equipment including canoes. To do this you should contact, preferably in advance of arrival, the Polish Tourist Society, 1 Maja Street 1, Augustow or at the Hostel Stary Folwark, Lake Wigry.

GIZYCKO

This is the lake centre most Polish holidaymakers and international tourists make for. Sited on Lake Niegocin —one of the larger lakes—and in easy reach of Lake Sniardwy whose fifty square miles of water make it Poland's largest lake and lovely Lake Mamry just a little smaller, we thought Gizycko a magnificent place for a lake holiday.

Though the town is dominated by an old castle (in which you will find a restaurant) we found it hard to tear ourselves away from the lakes and streams surrounded by woods and forests. To us Gizycko seemed a typical holiday town. There were some bright cafés and milk bars, restaurants and plenty of typical souvenir shops stacked with ornamental wooden plates, dressed dolls, wooden brooches, boxes and wood carvings.

If you fancy a few steamer trips, and the whole area is well worth exploring by water, you will find pleasure craft leaving from the landing stage just below the castle.

At the boat yards along the shores of Lake Niegocin, there are plenty of sailing craft for hire. However, before they will let you have a hire craft to take on to the lakes they make sure you are able to swim and they won't take your word for it. You have to prove the point by stripping off and plunging into the lake to show your paces. Great fun for those working in the boat yards. Still, we thought this an admirable precaution. After all most of the lakes are deep and some quite wide and by making sure people can swim and keep afloat in case of accidents fatalities have been very few.

The atmosphere of Gizycko is strictly nautical, and the streets are always filled with people in shorts, striped jerseys or some kind of nautical rig, and of course mostly young people. In any case you see few people of great age in Poland.

Though there are hotels, most visitors choose to stay in one of the holiday villages scattered around the lakes. There is quite a large holiday village a mile outside the town as well as a number of camping sites.

For a water holiday in the transparent, enchanted silent wonderland that to us will always be Mazuria, you could hardly do better than visit Gizycko. We like to remember it as a gay twentieth century holiday resort set in unspoiled timeless countryside.

INFORMATION FOR THOSE PLANNING TO STAY IN GIZYCKO

(1) *How to Get There*

Most people seemed to travel by coach, though you can go by train from Warsaw via Bialystok and Elk.

(2) *Hotels*

In 2nd Class Category. Hotel Mazurski (91 beds) Avenue Grunwaldzka 17. Phone 201.

Hotel Zamek (61 beds) Avenue Moniuszki 14. Phone 868.

(3) *Restaurants*

The Pojeziere which is in the old castle is the smart place to go.

KETRZYN

You will want to visit Ketrzyn twenty miles west of Gizycko, not necessarily to see the town with the old fourteenth century Jerzego Church built on the steep banks of the River Guber but to take a walk across the heath with its clumps of trees among the heather and with a few tiny lochans to reflect the billowing clouds.

It was here that Hitler had his famous 'wolf's lair' (Wolfschanze) from which he directed the Nazi battles against the Soviet Union. It was at this spot that the famous 'Generals' Bomb Plot' was put into effect.

On July 20th 1944 Colonel Stauffenberg who was very well known and often at Hitler's conference table entered the Wolfschanze and was quickly passed through the three gates in the high tension barbed wire fences, the only way across the minefields to the great concrete bunker camouflaged by trees.

Having placed his brief case with its bomb beneath the table where the Fuehrer and his immediate staff were working and where it could be guaranteed to do the most harm, Colonel Stauffenberg left the bunker as quickly and as easily as he had entered.

The plot failed through chance and the indecision of the conspirators. The brief case was accidently moved from the place where it had been left to behind a table leg and exploded, killing three men, wounding ten, bruising, singeing and infuriating the Fuehrer.

Colonel Stauffenberg hearing the explosion and assuming Hitler dead flew back to Berlin where things immediately began to go wrong. Many high-ranking conspirators refused to take decisive action, others made some half-hearted moves but were not so quick as the Nazis who before the end of the day rounded up Colonel Stauffenberg who with half a dozen other conspirators who had tried to seize the War Office was immediately shot.

Vengeance on the Generals found to be implicated was merciless. After a swift trial they were hung in a barbaric fashion from butcher's meat hooks, their death agonies being filmed and later screened for the Fuehrer.

This spot which was one of the nerve centres of the war, busy with the comings and goings of Generals and politicians, is now quite deserted. You can visit the blockhouse where Hitler spent so many hours poring over his maps. It has been smashed but is still impressive with the three-foot thick concrete slabs which covered the entrance.

Germans know this place as Rastenburg, but with the Liberation, Poland changed the German name to its

29. The Town Hall at Poznan

30. The Town Hall at Torun

31. The Town Hall at Wroclaw

32. The Renaissance church at Kazimierz Dolny on the Vistula

original Polish name—Ketrzyn.

As we walked back across the heath we wondered just why this place had been chosen. True it was in bleak, isolated country but surely this could not have been the only reason?

If you intend to motor from Ketrzyn to Olsztyn, take the road through Reszel and Lidzbark Warminski. You will find it to be a pleasant drive through the forests with views of many lakes.

RESZEL

This is an enchanting small town (population 3,500) captured in the thirteenth century by the Teutonic Knights who built the small attractive *castle* which with its cylindrical tower dominates the town.

The *market place* is bordered by many of the original houses, while the fifteenth century church with its vaulting and old crucifix is certainly worth getting out of the car to see.

A walk around the town is time well spent. It is full of little cobbled streets, and the great gabled houses are really beautiful, providing some wonderful camera shots. (Hotel Miejski—3rd Class Category—35 beds).

LIDZBARK WARMINSKI

Twenty-five miles north of Olsztyn on the edge of the Mazurian Lake District in lovely rural scenery, Lidzbark Warminski (population 11,000) has a small interesting *castle* which has been said to be the best preserved piece of mediaeval architecture in Poland—high praise indeed and as we found not altogether undeserved.

Reached by crossing a small bridge over what used to be the moat it is built around an arcaded courtyard with three graceful square towers, one at each corner, the fourth being taller and octagonal.

Inside is a chapel which glows with beautiful, coloured frescoes. The painting is rather primitive but the colours have withstood the passage of time quite remarkably.

If you happen to be motoring in the area it is worth making a detour to visit this castle.

In the town you will find a *fourteenth century gateway*, a *church* of the same period while all around the *market place* are the original merchants' houses many with attractive baroque fronts.

If you wish to stay in the town you will find accommodation in the Dom Wycieczkowy—2nd Class Category Tourist Hotel—(55 beds) in the Avenue Wysoka Brama, Phone 521.

OLSZTYN

With a population approaching 65,000 Olsztyn, straddling the River Lyna, is a good spot from which to explore the Mazurian countryside, especially if you are travelling by car. Not only do you have easy road access to the many eastern lakes, but you can also motor west to the smaller, lesser known lakes around Ostroda or south to lakes Lanskie and Pluszno.

We found the surrounding countryside with forested hills and rivers linking the lakes together most attractive and it will certainly not disappoint you should you choose to stay in Olsztyn.

Olsztyn seemed to be full of good things, though like so much else we had seen in Poland many of the things which caught your eye had been skilfully rebuilt after wartime destruction.

The *Town Hall* with its gables and tall tower reminded

us of similar buildings in Central Germany. It dominates the charming *Rynek* (market place) with its interesting arcaded houses.

Close to the Rynek is the *Wysoka Brama* or Great Gate, part of the original fourteenth century fortifications. It seemed rather odd to see trams passing under it. But it is better that it should adapt itself to twentieth century progress rather than be pulled down to make way for increasing traffic. Even its inside has been transformed into a popular tourist hotel. This has helped towards its preservation for this is in fact all that is left of the three walls which once encircled the town.

The *castle* found in Zamkowa Street was one of the great fourteenth century strongholds built by the Poles to stop the depredations of the Teutonic Knights who time and again besieged it. One of its defenders was the famous Bishop-astronomer Nicolaus Copernicus who during one of the Teutonic invasions held the castle against their superior forces.

The best view of the castle is across the Lyna River where you can appreciate its slender tower half-hidden by trees with a foreground of delightful half-timbered houses.

The castle walls enclose a small green courtyard, and we were rather taken by the red pantiled roof of the small porch which gives access to the first floor's vaulted rooms. In the porch our guide pointed out the fragments of a sundial said to have been designed by the famous astronomer Nicolaus Copernicus who lived in the castle for four years.

Part of the castle has been turned into the *Regional Museum* and though it has some interesting pieces it is by no means outstanding.

The *Fara Olsztynska* or parish church is also known as the cathedral. It looks sombre with its tall tower though we liked its ornamental gable. Built in the fourteenth century it has some Gothic vaulting but little else.

While in Olsztyn make the sixteen-mile trip to *Olsztynek*, a little town surrounded by wooded hills. Just before reaching the town which has a small *castle* you will see the *Skansen Park Museum*.

Like its Stockholm namesake it is full of village architecture collected together to display all that is best and most typical of the area.

There are old wooden windmills with large wooden sails, a little wooden church with a thatched roof brilliantly painted inside by peasant artists and wood carvers. There are cottages and farm buildings of all kinds as well as a manor house. This type of museum always appeals to us and we think to most tourists too.

Most Poles visiting Olsztynek continue south-west to view the battlefield of *Grunwald* (*Tannenberg*) where on July 15th 1410 the Polish king Ladislaw Jagiello with the help of ill-equipped levies from Russia, Lithuania and Czechoslovakia came up against a force of 20,000 magnificently armoured knights of the Teutonic Order and during a day of tremendous fighting defeated the Teutons so decisively that their enormous power was for ever broken.

Though the battlefield now has a monument put up at a spot which gives a wide view of the battle area there is little to see except the woods from which the Polish troops poured, the often marshy meadows and an occasional farm building.

An excursion of a different kind is from Olsztyn to the *Kanal Elblaski* (Elblag Canal) linking Ostroda with Elblag. Though we ourselves did not do this trip, it is unique.

Along certain stretches of the canal pleasure boats are

taken from the water and mounted on rollers across dry land, passing through woods and meadows until they reach the next stretch of navigable water.

This method was used by the Vikings to move their long boats across narrow stretches of land—and it could be that this method of transportation in Mazuria could date from sea-rover days.

INFORMATION FOR THOSE PLANNING TO STAY IN OLSZTYN

(1) *How to Get There*

You can travel from Poznan by train via Torun or by train from Warsaw. There are also coach services from both Poznan and Warsaw.

(2) *Hotels*

In 1st Class Category. Hotel Warminski (241 beds) Avenue Kosciuszki 49. Phone 526.

In 2nd Class Category. Hotel Nad Lyna (114 beds) Avenue Woj Polskiego 14. Phone 47-76.

In 2nd Class Category. Dom Wycieczkowy (110 beds) Avenue Swierczewskiego. Phone 51-50.

(3) *Restaurants*

Pod Zaglami, Pienieznego 22 or the Warszawska at Avenue Warszawska 16 are reasonably good ones.

(4) *Orbis*

Orbis have a travel and exchange office at Avenue Dabrowszczakow 8.

PART IX
OTHER PLACES OF INTEREST

POZNAN

KEY TO THE POZNAN MAP

H = Hotels
M = Museums

1. Town Hall and Museum of Instruments
2. City Walls (Fragments)
3. Parish Church
4. Bernadine Church
5. Corpus Christi Church
6. St. John's Church
7. The Cathedral
8. Dominican Church
9. St. Adalbert's Church
10. National Museum
11. Raczynski Library
12. St. Martin's Church
13. Archaeological Museum
14. New Town Hall
15. Opera
16. Poznan International Fair Ground
17. Botanical Gardens and Zoo
18. The Citadel

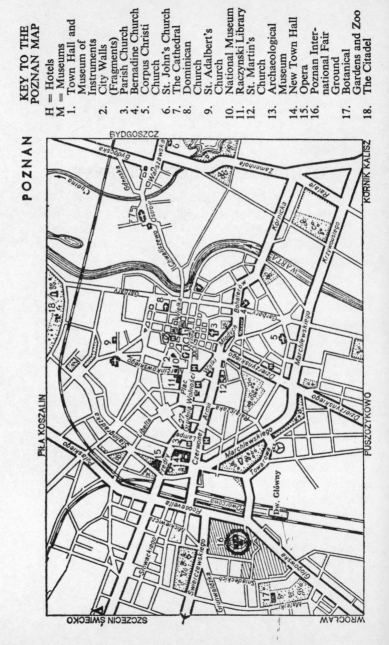

POZNAN

Poznan is the first major Polish city seen by tourists entering from the West.

Straddling the main trade routes between east and west, Poznan grew from a fortified village to become in the tenth century Poland's first capital. In the sixteenth century it had a population exceeding 20,000 and attracted many Italian artists and architects who set about making it one of Poland's most beautiful cities.

The Swedish invasions ended the city's prosperity. In the seventeenth century three weeks of Swedish bombardment left the city in ruins. During the period of the partitions Poznan was given to Prussia who set about Germanising it.

After 1918, reverting back to Poland, it became a leading industrial centre with an important trade fair. Following the 1939 invasion, Hitler in an attempt to completely Germanise the city deported thousands of Poles, settling Germans in Polish homes.

In January 1945, the advance of the Soviet–Polish armies liberated most of Poznan, though a garrison of 20,000 Germans having shut themselves into the fortress continued to fight resulting in many parts of the city being bombarded into heaps of rubble.

Therefore what you see is another Polish rebuilding miracle, especially in the older parts of the city which have been beautifully reconstructed and are now a quiet backwater, the new commercial sections having moved west of *Wolnosci Square* which is the ideal starting point from which to begin exploring the old city.

It is but a few steps from Wolnosci Square to the

241

Rynek—the old town market place.

Reconstruction has long been completed, and today with its old arcaded buildings colourwashed in blue, red, gold, and lilac it looks delightful though a little too spick and span.

Its more important houses include No. 78—the Dzialynski Palace. No. 91 the nineteenth century Miezynski Palace is now the Dom Turysty Hotel and No. 55 the *Museum of Musical Instruments*.

At its centre is the sixteenth century *Town Hall* containing the *Poznan Historical Museum* and the *Municipal Council Chamber* with a coffered ceiling decorated with coats of arms. In front of the Town Hall is the old pillory built from fines imposed on any woman considered to be too expensively dressed.

Cross to the south side of the Rynek and go along Swietoslawska Street to the *Old Parish Church* built between 1651 and 1705. Inside it is quite beautiful with very rich stucco work and wall and ceiling paintings. In its left aisle is a very interesting fifteenth century statue of 'Christ in Torment'.

The seventeenth century baroque *Church of the Franciscans* at the foot of the castle hill has paintings done by an eighteenth century friar, Adam Szwach, his talented brother Anthony carving the altar piece and the choir stalls.

The eighteenth century miniature portraits arranged above the Jesus Chapel are those placed on the coffins of nobility during their funeral processions.

Poznan Cathedral, found in Ostrow Tumski Street, though originally built in the tenth century suffered so extensively during the war that it had virtually to be rebuilt.

Like much of Poland's Gothic architecture it is largely built from red brick. Though its front with two slender towers may look ordinary enough, when seen from the rear, with its three side chapels with odd-shaped cupolas, it looks almost eastern.

You can visit the tenth century crypt, which has some vaulting and the remains of the tomb of Poland's first king, Mieszko I, founder of the Piast dynasty. Apart from the crypt, a sixteenth century triptych above the high altar and traces of fifteenth century frescoes there is little to be seen.

Anyone interested in plants might like to visit the *Botanical Gardens*—entrance in Matejki Avenue. One of the oldest gardens of its kind in Europe, it has more than 8,000 varieties of plants and a beautiful palm house.

Having looked at the old town, make your way to the modern section with its boulevards, apartment and office blocks, shops, cafés and general air of vitality. Here you can sense the rhythm which has put Poznan back on top.

From the tourist viewpoint, Poznan only seemed moderately interesting and having visited most of the principal places of interest in a half day, we had no urge to linger.

INFORMATION FOR THOSE PLANNING TO STAY IN POZNAN

(1) *How to Get There*

By through trains from Ostend or the Hook of Holland. It is also the terminal point for the express coaches operated by some British travel agents from Ostend and the Hook of Holland. Air travellers fly to Warsaw and continue on domestic flights.

(2) *Hotels*

In S Category. Hotel Merkury (653 beds) Avenue Roosevelt 20. Phone 472-31.

In 1st Class Category. Hotel Bazar (157 beds) Avenue Marcinkowskiego 10. Phone 512-51.

Hotel Wielkopolski (141 beds) Avenue Armii Czerwonej 67. Phone 80-31.

Hotel Poznanski (173 beds) Avenue Marcinkowskiego 22. Phone 81-21.

Hotel Lech (119 beds) Avenue Armii Czerwonej 74. Phone 82-31.

In 2nd Class Category. Hotel Staromiejski (68 beds) Avenue Rybaki 19. Phone 87-10.

Hotel Dom Turysty (276 beds) Stary Rynek 89/91. Phone 514-20.

In 3rd Class Category. Hotel Zacisze (54 beds) Avenue Armii Czerwonej 71. Phone 15-30.

(3) *Restaurants*

Arkadia—11, Wolnosci Square (Dancing).
W-Z—12, Avenue Fredry (Dancing).
Adria—14, Avenue Glogowska (Dancing).
Moulin Rouge—8, Avenue Hantaka (Dancing).

(4) *Cafés*

Wrzos—17, Wolnosci Square.
Savoy—6, Avenue Nowowiejskiego.
Literacka—Stary Rynek 46/47.

(5) *Museums*

National Museum. Avenue Marcinkowskiego 9. Devoted to fine arts.

Poznan Historical Museum. In the Town Hall, Stary Rynek.

Army Museum. Stary Rynek 9.
Museum of Musical Instruments. Stary Rynek 45.

(6) *Opera House*

St. Moniuszki—Avenue Fredry 9.

(7) Concert Hall

Philharmonic Hall—Avenue Armii Czerwonej 81.

(8) Twenty-four Hour Petrol Pump

The day and night service garage is in the Avenue Gwardii Ludowej, next door to the TOS motor repair service.

(9) Orbis

The Orbis office for the booking of excursions and currency exchange is at Avenue Marcinkowskiego 11.

WROCLAW

Wroclaw—better known by its German name, Breslau—is sited on the River Oder (Odra) in the centre of the rich Silesian Province.

It has had a chequered history, passing from Polish into Czech, Prussian and German hands. It has been captured, its populations decimated by butchery and disease. It has been burned down only to be rebuilt and at times almost taxed out of existence. Yet somehow it managed to survive to become a treasure house of beautiful monuments, until the last war almost wiped it from the map for ever.

On February 12th 1945 with the victorious Soviet–Polish armies pressing close to the German frontier, the German Chief of Staff for Lower Silesia together with Gauleiter Hanke decided to make Wroclaw, which had a German garrison of 40,000 men, a fortress. Hemming in the 400,000 German citizens still in the town the city was turned into a strongpoint, its centre, including two old churches, being torn down to make a landing strip to which reinforcements could be flown from Berlin.

The siege lasted almost three months. Though

bombed, shelled, mortared and shot at, the garrison held out until the 6th May 1945 when Berlin had fallen and Wroclaw was nothing more than rubble. The landing strip was only used once, to fly Gauleiter Hanke from a city of corpses.

Wroclaw's defence had cost more than 300,000 dead, the total destruction of 75 per cent of all buildings. Some districts had been wiped out completely. In the industrial section 60 per cent of the plants had been totally destroyed and 30 per cent so badly damaged as to be almost useless. Once a city of 600,000 people, by the end of 1945 with most of its German population dead or fled, the total population had shrunk to 30,000 most of whom were Poles. Today, Wroclaw's population is 460,000 and once again it is a prosperous city with large textile and chemical factories, engineering and metallurgical works and film studios.

The first rebuilding was concentrated on the old city which today looks very much as it did before 1939. Its architectural gem is the *Gothic Town Hall* standing in the centre of the old market place—the *Rynek*.

The Town Hall has a beautiful sixteenth century gable covered with sculptures and friezes to give it a beautiful lace-like appearance. This does not mean the rest of the building is ordinary. Everywhere you look are loggias and turrets, while the tall slender tower with its sixteenth century clock is a lovely thing.

Inside it is no less interesting with its fourteenth century wine cellar, while some of the rooms with their lovely ornamented doorways and collections of sixteenth and seventeenth century furniture are delightful.

Part of the building is devoted to the *Historical Museum* which has a collection of rare Silesian coins from the eleventh–eighteenth centuries.

Around the Rynek are reconstructed sixteenth century

merchants' houses which with their richly decorated fronts and gables make a perfect setting for the Town Hall.

Wroclaw Cathedral built on the Ostrow Tumski—which in Polish means cathedral island—is reached by crossing the River Oder. A city backwater, its churches set around with flower gardens are half hidden among the trees.

The cathedral was almost wiped out during the 1945 siege, the Germans using it to store ammunition, but after five years of painstaking labour it was restored, much of its shattered stonework being pieced together like a giant jigsaw.

Close by is the *Holy Cross Church* built in the thirteenth century and containing a series of mediaeval sculptures.

Though Wroclaw does have beautiful things, in the main it is a bustling industrial city which we are glad to have seen, though we had little desire to linger longer than necessary.

INFORMATION FOR THOSE PLANNING TO STAY IN WROCLAW

(1) *How to Get There*

By through train from Ostend or the Hook of Holland to Poznan and then on by local train. Wroclaw has a domestic airport with connections to Warsaw and Gdansk.

(2) *Hotels*

In S Category. Hotel Orbis Monopol (134 beds) Avenue Modrzejewskiej 2. Phone 370-41.

Hotel Grand (262 beds) Avenue Swierczewskiego 102/104. Phone 360-71.

In 1st Class Category. Hotel Polonia (254 beds) Avenue Swierczewskiego 66/7. Phone 350-81.

In 2nd Class Category. Hotel Europejski (190 beds) Avenue Swierczewskiego. Phone 387-39.

Hotel Odra (103 beds) Avenue Stawowa 13. Phone 375-60.

Hotel Piast (125 beds) Avenue Swierczewskiego 96/98. Phone 372-28.

(3) *Restaurants*

KDL—Kosciuszki Square 5/6 (Dancing).
Klubowa—Avenue Doroty 16 (Dancing).

(4) *Cafés*

Sezam—Avenue Swierczewskiego 65 (Music).

(5) *Shopping*

You can buy everything you want in the shops around Kosciuszki Square.

(6) *Orbis*

The Orbis excursion and exchange office is at Avenue Swierczewskiego 60/62.

CZESTOCHOWA

With a population of 158,000 and one of Poland's leading industrial centres with a smelting works and textile factories, Czestochowa is Poland's sacred city, with the *Jasna Gora Monastery* its only notable building, a centre of religious pilgrimage.

In the monastery, first erected in the fourteenth and reconstructed and extended in the seventeenth and eighteenth centuries, is the portrait of *Our Lady of Czestochowa* said to have been painted by St. Luke, but in actual fact the work of an obscure fourteenth century Italian.

During the Swedish Wars the monastery was besieged by the Swedish army and in danger of capture. When everything seemed lost, legend has it that the virgin in the painting came to the aid of the defenders who continued to fight.

Their heroic struggle so impressed the Poles who had considered the war lost, that they rose up against the invaders and turned defeat into victory.

The Poles point out that no matter what disasters have befallen Czestochowa the painting has never been harmed. One soldier trying to steal the picture found it could not be moved and when in anger he struck it with his sword, blood is supposed to have flowed from the picture.

Though August is the time for the great pilgrimages to the city, you can see the picture any morning provided you get up early and attend the six o'clock mass.

A golden door hides the painting which is above an altar draped with jewels and precious gifts given to the virgin by generations of pilgrims.

During early mass, to a fanfare of trumpets the golden door hiding the painting opens for everyone to see the picture. This is a tense emotional moment which impresses everyone who experiences it making a visit to Czestochowa more than worthwhile.

If you wish to stay in the city, there is a 1st Class Category Hotel—the Centralny—in the Avenue Swierczewskiego.

KAZIMIERZ DOLNY

Kazimierz Dolny (population 10,000) is a town of seventeenth century importance which slowly died, but retained its old monuments to become something of a Polish showpiece.

Its wealth was based on the shipments of grain from the rich countryside around Lublin, down the Vistula to Gdansk. At the end of the sixteenth century when most of the buildings you see were built, Kazimierz Dolny was at the height of its prosperity.

When Poland was partitioned, cut off from Gdansk, its commercial importance ended. Severe war damage has been repaired and today Kazimierz Dolny delights everyone who sees it. Even the touring coaches in the market place cannot take away the eye-catching loveliness of the *Przybyla family house*.

Above a series of six arcades were the living quarters of two families—the brothers Nicolas and Christopher Przybyla sharing the same house. The square-leaded windows looking on to the market place are surrounded by rich stone carving. One features St. Nicholas with his crozier, the other St. Christopher with the child Jesus on his shoulders.

The living quarters are topped off by 'Polish attics' rich with mouldings of saints and medallions. I doubt whether Poland has another house quite so lovely as this.

The *Celezowska house* set among the trees of Senetorska Street overlooking the tiny Grodarz stream is equally lovely. The lower half of the house is not so ornate, though the cornices with all kinds of monsters like dragons and griffins are extraordinarily beautiful when seen against the egg-shell blue sky.

You can spend hours wandering around this little town which is a treasure house of sixteenth century Polish domestic architecture. The *church* is certainly worth some of your time and a climb up to the fourteenth century *castle* provides a view of the countryside and river.

The market place is the centre of attraction though it is something of a shock to find the cinema in the old *eighteenth century synagogue*. Do see the enormous *seventeenth century granaries* and the *monastery* which also help make Kazimierz Dolny a truly delightful place worth making a special journey to see.

INFORMATION FOR THOSE PLANNING TO STAY IN KAZIMIERZ DOLNY

(1) *How to Get There*

By train from Warsaw to Pulawy, then by local bus or Vistula steamer.

(2) *Hotels*

In 2nd Class Category. Hotel Miejski (18 beds) Rynek 12. Phone 4.

In 3rd Class Category. Dom Wycieczkowy. Avenue Krakowska 61. Phone 61. This hotel is in one of the old seventeenth century granaries which has been converted to provide accommodation for 204 guests.

LUBLIN

Lublin (population 188,000) an industrial and university city escaped major war damage.

Sited on an important mediaeval trade route linking Lithuania with Bohemia and mid-way between the rivers Bug and Vistula, Lublin quickly grew in importance and by the fourteenth century, dominated by its castle and surrounded by ramparts to keep out the Tartars who constantly threatened it, Lublin was one of Poland's strongest and most prosperous cities, rival to Cracow which we thought it resembled in many ways.

251

When Casimir the Great opened Poland to the Jews many settled in Lublin. At the time of the Nazi invasion, Lublin had one of the largest Jewish communities in Poland living in the old part of the city or in the surrounding villages in varying degrees of poverty and squalor. In 1939 in some East Polish towns as many as 90 per cent of the population were Jewish.

A prosperous and splendid city, Lublin was visited by most Polish kings who stayed in the magnificent castle which at times was used for meetings of the Polish Parliament.

In the seventeenth century Lublin's tide of prosperity was halted. The Swedish invasions and the Cossack Wars did not help the city and though an increasing population caused it to spread beyond its ramparts the majority of citizens living just above subsistence level had a pretty thin time.

The Nazis dealt harshly with Lublin, many citizens, especially Jews, dying in the big extermination camp set up outside the city.

Being near the Soviet border, Lublin was one of the first Polish cities to be liberated. The Nazis not having decided the pattern of total destruction for Polish cities before evacuation, the victorious Russian–Polish army marched into a virtually untouched city. For six months, until Warsaw was liberated, Lublin was the capital of Free Poland.

Begin your sightseeing at the *castle* which, set on its hill above the narrow twisting streets of the old town, dominates the entire city.

Recently restored, the castle is quite interesting with its fourteenth century keep with typical spiral staircases remodelled in the nineteenth century. The *castle chapel*, its nave supported on a single pillar and with frescoes painted in the fifteenth century by Ruthenian artists, is particularly beautiful and interesting.

Leaving the castle pass through the dark passage way of the *Brama Grodzka* (City Gate) once connected to the castle by a drawbridge. A city strongpoint, today it looks no more than a house cut through with an archway leading to a tiny square.

You now enter a warren of streets and alleys lined with sixteenth, seventeenth and eighteenth century houses, many with moulded fronts and ornamental doorways which collectively form the old town where Lublin's large pre-war Jewish population lived.

Wandering through these old streets you will today hardly see one bearded, black-caftaned Jew or youth with ceremonial curls and virgin beard which before 1939 were common to this quarter.

Look at the *Church of St. Stanislaus* at the corner of Klonowicza Street, with its bell tower covered with decorations and its eleven side chapels. That known as the *Kaplica Firlejowska* with its cupola decorated with rich stucco ornamentation is glorious, though many prefer the seventeenth century *Tyskiewicz Kaplica* whose cupola is ornamented by a magnificent fresco depicting Judgement Day. This is certainly a building which must not be missed.

For such a large city the *Rynek*—market place—is surprisingly small. Surrounded by the original houses, many with rich decorations, especially No. 12 known as the *Sobieski House* in which both Charles XII of Sweden and Peter the Great of Russia lived, it is full of charm.

The centre of the market is dominated by the eye-catching eighteenth century *Town Hall* which apart from its size has little to offer.

The old town is full of interesting seventeenth and eighteenth century stucco ornamented churches, fine examples of their type but not to everyone's taste. The *Brama Krakowska*—Cracow Gate—with its sturdy square crenellated walls cut through by a dark archway and behind it a high rectangular clock tower is worth seeing.

We enjoyed walking in the old town looking in the tiny shop windows or staring at passers-by, many of them peasants from the surrounding villages. My wife was much taken with their bright woollen headscarves which seemed so typically Polish, but turned out to be of Japanese manufacture.

Lublin was Poland as we had always imagined it. Old, different, slightly down at heel, but immensely colourful, a complete contrast to the *Krakowskie Przedmiescie*, the modern boulevard leading to big *Litowski Square*, the commercial heart of modern Lublin and on to the *University* and *Municipal Park*.

A stay in Lublin is incomplete without a quick visit to the *Majdanek extermination camp* two miles from the city centre.

The atrocities of Auschwitz have overshadowed the horrors of Majdanek in which $1\frac{1}{2}$ million people died. When in 1945 the human ashes surrounding the crematorium were collected they reached to a height of thirty feet.

Though you will find much of the camp has been turned into a parklike cemetery, some of the original buildings together with the crematoria furnaces have been kept as a museum. If you have not seen Auschwitz, make a point of seeing Majdanek.

INFORMATION FOR THOSE PLANNING TO STAY IN LUBLIN
(1) *How to Get There*

There are direct coach services and rail links between Warsaw and Lublin.

(2) *Hotels*

In 1st Class Category. Hotel Lublinianska (119 beds) Avenue Krakowskie Przedmiescie 56. Phone 63-25.

In 2nd Class Category. Hotel Europa (228 beds) Avenue Krakowskie Przedmiescie. Phone 77-56.

In 3rd Class Category. Hotel Polonia (79 beds) Avenue I Armii W.P. 5. Phone 31-07.

Tourist Hotel. Dom Wycieczkowy (174 beds) Litewski Square 2. Phone 81-07.

(3) *Restaurants*

Those in the hotels Europa and Lublinianska are popular as they have bands for dancing.

(4) *Orbis*

There is an Orbis office with a currency exchange bureau at Krakowskie Przedmiescie 29.

TORUN

On the drive from Poznan to Warsaw it is worth making the detour to Torun, taking in some of the lakes en route.

Torun, half-way between Warsaw and Gdansk, is recognised as the birthplace of the great prelate-astronomer Nicolaus Copernicus and has much to offer those who go there.

An important fourteenth century city, a member of the powerful Hanseatic League, today it is still commercially active with several factories.

However, the twentieth century has not been allowed to interfere with its old world charm and as you wander the quiet streets of the old city it is possible to slip back in time quite easily. Spared wartime ravages, it is a treasure house of old buildings, especially the *Rynek* with its fourteenth century *Gothic Town Hall* whose tower was built much earlier. The thirteenth century *Church of St. John* has some fourteenth century stained glass. You can still see the house in which Copernicus was born, as well as the fourteenth century town walls with their gatehouses and turrets.

There are two 1st Class Category hotels—the Pod Orlem in Mostowa Avenue and the Polonia in Armii Czerwonej Square 5.

SANDOMIERZ

Between Lublin and Cracow, Sandomierz is one of Poland's oldest and most interesting towns. Lucky enough to escape major war damage, it is full of old buildings including an old town gate—*Brama Opatowska* —a *Town Hall*, parts of which date from the thirteenth century, a fourteenth century *cathedral* with frescoes as well as many fifteenth century houses. In fact the whole town is redolent of the past.

Exploring Sandomierz we found the hours passed quickly, but before we left we did spare sufficient time to drive south to *Lancut Palace* with its *Coach Museum, a seventeenth century synagogue and ornamental gardens.*

Had time permitted we would have liked to have sailed down the Vistula to Kazimierz Dolny. But half the trouble of holidaying in a country like Poland is that there is so very much to see.

We certainly found our sightseeing rewarding, because we found the Poles were really fond of their old buildings, spending time and money on careful restoration and preservation.

There's so much going on in Poland today, that it seems to change its face almost overnight. But any woman will tell you a change of face does not mean a change of character. And so it is with Poland, a country whose character is quite unique.

INDEX

260

261